Karen Bulley is the Pilots Develo [...]
Church and Moderator of the C [...]
Among Children (CGMC). A ke [...]
is to write programme and resource materials for 5–18s for Pilots,
*which sits within the United Reformed Church and works with several
denominations including the Methodist Church, Baptist Church,
Congregational Federation, Church of England, Church of Scotland and
the Church in Wales.*

    *Her published material includes contributions for publications
such as* Partners in Learning *and, more recently,* CORE Skills for
Children's Work, *for which she is part of the management group. As
Pilots Development Officer for the United Reformed Church, Karen is
responsible for a minimum of two publications each year for use with
children, one based on worship and the other on the study of a country.
She either writes or edits the material, which always includes theme-
based ideas for crafts, worship, activities, games and theme exploration.
Karen also writes articles and magazine pieces and is involved with
training adults to work with children and young people.*

    Karen lives in Hampshire with her family and six chickens.

Text copyright © Karen Bulley 2010
The author asserts the moral right
to be identified as the author of this work

**Published by
The Bible Reading Fellowship**
15 The Chambers, Vineyard
Abingdon OX14 3FE
United Kingdom
Tel: +44 (0)1865 319700
Email: enquiries@brf.org.uk
Website: www.brf.org.uk
BRF is a Registered Charity

ISBN 978 1 84101 663 4

First published 2010
10 9 8 7 6 5 4 3 2 1 0

Acknowledgments
Unless otherwise stated, scripture quotations are taken from the Contemporary English
Version of the Bible published by HarperCollins Publishers, copyright © 1991, 1992, 1995
American Bible Society.

Scripture quotations taken from the Holy Bible, New International Version, copyright © 1973,
1978, 1984 by International Bible Society, are used by permission of Hodder & Stoughton
Publishers, a division of Hodder Headline Ltd. All rights reserved. 'NIV' is a registered
trademark of International Bible Society. UK trademark number 1448790.

A catalogue record for this book is available from the British Library

Printed in Singapore by Craft Print International Ltd

Creative Ideas for
All-Age Church

12 through-the-year programmes for informal
church services and special one-off events

Karen Bulley

*

This book is dedicated to Peter, Jim and Sam,
who are my constant inspiration.　　　　*

Acknowledgments

Thank you to Leo Roberts, my good friend and often writing companion, for his invaluable help in bouncing ideas around, and to Huw Morrison and Soo Webster for their enthusiasm, guidance and wisdom with proofreading. Thank you also to Sue Doggett at BRF, who helped me to believe that this book was possible, and to the many who, through their love and friendship, have helped me to achieve the many things I have.

Without the constant support and encouragement of my family and friends, this book could not have been written.

Contents

Foreword		6
Introduction		7
Theme 1	A to Z of what we offer	15
Theme 2	Let the water flow	26
Theme 3	One body, one meal, one church	36
Theme 4	Celebrate life	49
Theme 5	Patchwork stories	59
Theme 6	Beautiful prayer	71
Theme 7	The wheels on the bus…	83
Theme 8	Quiet places	94
Theme 9	Fruit cocktail	105
Theme 10	Surviving the storm	114
Theme 11	Following traditions	125
Theme 12	Christmas	139
Bible index		152
Resources		153

*

Foreword

Church is about meeting God. God meets us in Jesus through the words of the Bible, through worship and the sacraments, and through each other. Some find God easily in cathedrals and churches where the worship is dignified, beautiful and formal. Others find that kind of atmosphere difficult and respond better to a different, less formal, more relaxed way of being church. This book is for people who are trying to 'do' church in that kind of way.

All-age church is relaxed church—a different kind of space from 'traditional' church—but that doesn't mean it's 'sloppy' church; nor (as this book makes clear) is it 'unliturgical'.

Liturgy is about the rhythm of life and the movement of the year. One of the gifts this book offers is a sense of that movement. Each chapter begins with a meditation on the mood of the month and its links with the feasts, fasts and festivals of the Christian year. So we begin in Epiphany and journey through Lent, Easter and Ordinary Time to Christmas. Those rhythms are as important to all-age church as they are to the grandest cathedral.

Good all-age church makes considerable demands on its leaders because it requires constant creativity, so we can be grateful to Karen Bulley for the rich diet of ideas for all ages that she has laid out for us. All are accompanied by sensible practical planning advice which, importantly, also covers compliance with the legislation on working with children and young people. Most importantly, though, these ideas are the product of a grounded, thoughtful, mature Christian faith.

What we have, in short, is a complete tool kit for all-age church. So enjoy it, be creative, make spaces where God can be encountered, and to God be the praise and the glory.

David Cornick, General Secretary, Churches Together in England

*

Introduction

This book is based on the simple belief that, in order to grow as part of God's family, churches need to learn to play together as well as working and worshipping together. By playing together, the church family shares experiences in a way that more formal worship situations do not allow. Once people begin to share in this way, their worship and involvement with the Christian message will be enriched.

Creative Ideas for All-Age Church is a book of themes and ideas that can be used in a variety of situations. It is not a selection of notes for sermon writing or Bible study and it is not a book of activities to be used only with the younger members of the church. This book is for the whole church family and is best suited to an informal church setting such as a café-style situation. It contains a series of journeys—through the calendar year and the Christian year and through themes that can be embraced at any time of year.

The twelve themes in this book contain a mixture of creative worship ideas, all designed to encourage the worshipping community to listen to the thoughts and stories of those in their midst. Most of the activities are suitable for all ages together, but there are also some age-specific activities. The age suggestions are guidelines based on probable ability but can be used by others, too. Through listening and worshipping together in this way, we promote a deeper respect and understanding, an increase in creative thinking and, at times, a need for vulnerability, all of which will help people of all ages to grow in faith together.

This general introduction includes the rationale behind the concept, suggestions for using the material and guidelines on how to run each theme, either for a once-a-month informal service or as a one-off special event. The programmes could also be built into a church weekend or residential time away. Advice is given on the preparation needed and some general guidance on what can be achieved by using the material.

The themes can be used to design stand-alone worship programmes or to follow the pattern of the Christian year through a once-a-month exploration of the colour, creativity and individuality of each season. The themes themselves are only the starting point and the material in this book should be supplemented with thoughts and other activities that will work within the local situation. The themes range from those that are based on a particular Bible passage through to issues relevant to the church family and abstract ideas designed to promote lateral thinking or just for fun.

How to use the themes

The material offers a wide range of practical ideas and activities designed to give choice to those planning the worship. This means that a pick-and-mix approach can be used, to tailor the worship to the needs of those participating.

Most of the themes follow a set structure and include the following sections:

- Suggested month, season of the year, Christian season and colour
- Theme introduction
- Biblical context and reflection
- Theme exploration
- Age-specific theme activities
- Sharing a meal together
- Ideas for reflection, prayer and sung worship
- Taking it further

Some themes differ slightly from the outline above, but all include most of the elements.

Suggested month, season of the year, Christian season and colour

Each theme has a title, a suggestion for the month and season of the year in which it might be used, and an associated Christian season and liturgical colour. Themes are not necessarily based on the Christian seasons, although there may be references to the appropriate Christian season in the text. More can be made of the Christian season by adding ideas from other resources. The liturgical colour is given for those who wish to enhance their worship by using colour.

Theme introduction

This section has two purposes. The first is to remind us of what is happening in the natural world around us, by reflecting on the month and season in which the theme is set. The theme introduction encourages us to remember that our worship is set against the backdrop of God's natural world, which has its own routine, its own seasonal cycle and its own influence on what we do and how we think. Local and national geography, as well as climatic conditions, will affect the timing of the natural cycle and what is observed in the world around.

The second purpose is to introduce the theme for the worship and to set it in the context of our everyday lives.

Biblical context and reflection

All the themes have a biblical context, with a reflection or exposition on the text. Most of the themes offer the biblical passage first, followed by the reflection. Some themes have Bible passages interwoven as activities and passages are explored with a different approach. The Contemporary English Version of the Bible has been used throughout, unless stated otherwise.

Theme exploration

This section both expands on the biblical context and explores the theme through a mixture of activities, games and discussion starters. Although the activities are suggested under particular themes, most are transferrable between themes: if an activity works well in one situation, you could use it again in a different context. The theme exploration activities are suitable for all ages.

Age-specific theme activities

Most of these activities include a general age group suggestion. This is only a guideline to help with planning, as everyone has different abilities, which are specific to individuals and not to age. Most of the activities for younger age groups could be used with older groups. Activities for older groups could work with younger people but would need to be approached in a different way to ensure that everyone has the opportunity to explore the theme fully.

Sharing a meal together

Eating and drinking are social activities and feature frequently in the Bible. Gathering for a meal of some kind is relaxing and enables conversation to flow in a different way than it does in more formal settings. In this way, people get to know each other better.

The suggestions are provided to stimulate thinking and promote further ideas. All ages can be involved in preparing and sharing a meal and all can participate in it. Be mindful of health and safety, and take care to discover any food allergies that might exist in the group.

Sharing a meal or drinks together will take some time, but it is time well worth spending.

Ideas for reflection, prayer and sung worship

These are ideas to enhance the practical application of the theme material. When planning the worship, it is good to have quiet meditative times along with active busy times. This section makes additional suggestions for meditation and poetry as well as giving thematic ideas for prayers and hymns.

Taking it further

Guidelines are given to facilitate further action or thinking. Some themes naturally lend themselves towards this outcome. Some themes might actually effect change, which will need to be managed carefully and sensitively. At other times the church family, having enjoyed spending time together to worship informally, might decide to do something different in the future or seek to create more space in which they can gather together to follow a theme.

Planning ahead

A number of the themes include sections with the heading 'Plan ahead'. This indicates preparation that needs to take place during the previous week or another period of time before the worship is to take place.

Simple writing and drawing equipment is needed for many of the themes, such as coloured pens or pencils, collage materials, glue, scissors and sheets of paper. Keep these items ready in a box so that they don't need to be collected each time. Specific items needed for individual activities are listed where they are relevant.

Bringing it all together

Each theme has a number of threads, and the group planning the worship will need to decide which thread the worship is to follow. When a theme has been chosen, read it through thoroughly. Decide how much time is available for the worship and then decide where the worship will take place.

- Think about the structure of the worship. Decide if there are to be hymns or songs, when the biblical context will be read, and whether the prayers will be found in a published source, written beforehand or spoken as an impromptu part of the worship as the Holy Spirit leads.
- Think about the display and what needs to be gathered. Think about how the display will enhance the worship experience for everyone.
- Discuss with others who will be involved; make sure they know what is to happen and what they might need to prepare.
- If music is needed, ensure that plenty of notice is given to the organist, music group or whoever is responsible for providing the music.
- Use your knowledge of those in the worshipping community to aid the planning of the worship.

Groupwork guidelines

Groups should be of a manageable size and appropriate to the activity for which they are being used. For discussion-based activities, the groups should be small (around six to eight people) to enable everyone to share their opinions.

If mixed age groups are needed, try to have more than one member of several age groups in one group so that everyone feels comfortable and confident. For example, in a group of four, have two teenagers and two people in their 40s, rather than one nine-year-old, one teenager, one 40-year-old and someone in their 60s.

Respect with confidence

We are not all at the same starting point on our Christian journeys. For those who have been journeying a long time, the themes in this book will refresh their thinking; for others, the journey may have only just begun. Younger members may well be further along their journey than older members but may not have been able to share their wisdom and insights with others, and older members may have begun their journey a long time ago and no longer feel they have anything to share. Some are yet to decide whether a journey of faith is the road they want to take.

Wherever we are on our personal faith journey, we can look around and see others journeying on their own paths. We should be respectful of everyone on the paths and, when we can, we should aim to spend time walking alongside one another, sharing experiences, knowledge, surprise and wonder as we discover familiar paths and new turnings.

Key to songs

The songs listed in each chapter are taken from the following books:

- *Complete Junior Praise* (JP), Peter Horrobin and Greg Leavers (Collins, ISBN 978 0 00 725978 6)
- *Complete Mission Praise* (MP), Peter Horrobin and Greg Leavers (Collins, ISBN 978 0 00 719343 1)
- *Church Hymnary* (CH) (Canterbury Press, ISBN 978 1 85311 832 6)
- *Hymns Ancient & Modern New Standard* (HAM) (Canterbury Press, ISBN 978 0 90754 739 6)
- *Hymns & Psalms* (HP) (Methodist Publishing House, ISBN 978 0 946550 00 5)

- *Love from Below* (LB), John Bell & Graham Maule (The Iona Community, ISBN 978 0 947988 34 0)
- *Rejoice and Sing* (RS) (Oxford University Press, ISBN 978 0 19 146922 0)
- *The Source* (TS), Graham Kendrick (Kevin Mayhew, ISBN 978 1 84003 121 8)

*

— Theme 1 —

A to Z of what we offer

Suggested month
January

Season of the year
Winter

Christian season
Epiphany

Colour
White or gold

Theme introduction

January brings a mixture of dull, short days and bright, cold days, with a weak winter sun making trees and buildings into silhouettes. Everything can look weary and tired, yet there is such delight in waking to find a blanket of snow on the ground. Frozen puddles, frost-tipped leaves and icicles on the guttering have their own beauty and cause us to look afresh at the familiar sleeping world around us. January is the month when clear, dark skies are filled with bright stars and, if we manage to get a little distance away from street lamps, we can see so many of them.

It is good to look around us in the life of the church, too. After the colours of Christmas—the baubles, twinkling lights and vibrant poinsettias—after the sounds, sights and smells of celebration and the feeling of calm reassurance we get when we gaze at the wonder of the baby lying in the stable, it is easy to feel less than enthusiastic when we come back to our worship homes in January.

This is the time of Epiphany, the time when we remember wise men (or magi) travelling from their homes in the east, following a new star that leads them to the king for whom they have brought gifts. 'Epiphany' is from a Greek word that means 'manifestation' or 'appearance'. The wise men had studied the stars for years and recognised the signs that pointed to the extraordinary birth of a new and different kind of leader. They embarked on an epic journey to bring their gifts to the baby king. They brought gifts of material wealth and they brought gifts of their time and wisdom.

'A to Z of what we offer' helps people to consider and reflect on the gifts that they have. Maybe our gifts have been frozen or are sleeping like the winter landscape, or maybe we have not realised they are there at all. The activities in this section should help us to discover them anew. They are designed to be light-hearted and fun, creating an atmosphere of self-awareness and discovery that will enable us to appreciate the gifts we find in ourselves, to see the gifts in others and to look constructively at how those gifts might be used in the general life of the local church and its community.

Biblical context

A body is made up of many parts, and each of them has its own use. That's how it is with us. There are many of us, but we are each part of the body of Christ, as well as part of one another. God has also given each of us different gifts to use. If we can prophesy, we should do it according to the amount of faith we have. If we can serve others, we should serve. If we can teach, we should teach. If we can encourage others, we should encourage them. If we can give, we should be generous. If we are leaders, we should do our best. If we are good to others, we should do it cheerfully.
ROMANS 12:4–8

Reflection

Read the Bible passage through, either as a whole group or in smaller groups.

In the passage, Paul seems to be saying things that are obvious. He is saying, 'Do what you're naturally good at and don't try to be something you're not.' It sounds fairly simple and straightforward.

But Paul is saying more than that. He says that the gifts we have been given come with the grace of God (v. 6). In the Bible, the word 'grace' is used to mean different things, and in this context Paul is using it in the sense of an enabling power. He is telling his readers that if God has given them a gift, then God has also given them the ability to use it.

It is helpful to know that we have within us the ability to use the gifts that God has given us, but not everyone is able to recognise their own gift or gifts or to see how they can be used. Some people are able to see others' gifts better than their own.

Theme exploration

To set the scene, have a display area draped with a white or gold cloth. Add something that relates to the world around us, such as a picture of icicles or frosted cobwebs, or items that help to keep us warm, such as hats, scarves and gloves.

Quick discussion

This activity can be done in age-specific groups or in small groups of mixed ages, whichever feels more appropriate with your church.

Give each group a card on which is written the following question: 'What gifts would you have liked the wise men to bring to Mary, Joseph or Jesus?'

Allow each group five minutes to discuss this question.

Gifts, skills and talents

This activity is to be done in small groups around a table or with a table nearby, and is suitable for all ages working together. Some members of the group may need the help of others.

Make available a pile of plain A6-sized cards or postcards. (The backs of the pictures of used greetings cards could also be used.) Put the cards on the table with a pot of pens.

Several questions will be asked, and people are invited to write or draw their responses on the cards (one answer on each card). Ask them to write their own name on all the cards they use, to make it clear, when the cards are put together, which talents and gifts belong to whom. All responses are to be valued; for some, this task will be very challenging, so take care to present it in a caring way. Tell the group that the cards will be read out or shown later.

- Ask everyone to write or draw something they are naturally good at—for example, getting dressed, organising things, eating, reading, being on time, riding a bike and so on.
- Ask everyone to write or draw a talent they have been given, such as singing, dancing, playing sport of some kind, needlecraft, creating new recipes and so on.
- Ask everyone to write or draw something they are good at in church, such as reading from the Bible, making refreshments, being cheerful, handling the money, spring cleaning, arranging the books, having new ideas, decorating the church, running a group and so on. Try to encourage people to think beyond the Sunday worship.

Now ask everyone to think of the gifts, skills and talents of others in the small group and write or draw them on a card. Again, one gift only should be written on each card, but as many cards as are needed may be used. If members of the group do not know one another very well, they may need to start a conversation that will help them find out more about each other. The point of this part of the exercise is to help everyone to recognise the gifts that they cannot see for themselves. The cards should be personal and written in a positive way—for example, 'Arthur makes me smile' or 'Belinda is a talented flower arranger'. It might be appropriate to include people who are not present at the activity but are usually part of the worshipping community.

When both tasks have been completed, spread the cards face up on the table for all to see. Have ready a 'title' card for each small group with the words 'Our gifts, skills and talents' written on it. Place this in the centre of the cards.

When all the groups have finished the task, encourage everyone to walk around the room, viewing each other's tables to see what talents and gifts are within the whole church.

Task list

This activity is suitable for all ages working together.

Working in small groups, construct a list on a large piece of paper, either with words or pictures, of the tasks that need doing in your church. Some tasks will be obvious and will already be part of local church life—for example, cleaning the church, collecting hymn books, banking the offertory or buying refreshments. Other tasks might be new ideas to be considered—for example, establishing a worship group to help plan worship through the year, forming and coordinating a music group or worship band, designing a prayer board, creating a church website or baking cakes. This is a good opportunity to encourage fresh thinking.

Some members of the group may need help to participate in this activity, either because they are not able to write or draw, or because they are not sure how far it is acceptable to stretch their thinking. If people are more comfortable working in twos or threes, they should feel free to do so.

Match-making

Now, using the cards from the 'Gifts, skills and talents' activity and the 'Task list' you have just compiled, match the tasks to the people with the gifts and skills to fulfil them. NB: If there is not enough time to complete this activity during the worship time, it could be completed by a small group at another time.

You may find that, over the whole group, several people have the gifts needed to fulfil each task. This is good, as many tasks need more than one person to share the load, and there is always a need for a succession of new people with the identified talents to take over from current task holders when they are ready to move on. Not everyone finds it easy to move on from a task that they have been doing for a while, and some may need to be sensitively helped to see that the time is right for them to do so. Moving on is not negative in itself and should be approached positively; it can be liberating, providing an opportunity for other doors to open. We should care for each other pastorally when the time comes to change to other roles or to rest for a while.

Find a useful way to organise the information gained from the 'match-making' and get everyone's agreement that this can be done.

Some people may have the gifts required for a certain task, but their circumstances make them unable to take up the task when they are first asked. If this is the case, perhaps they will be happy to remain on the list to await a future invitation.

Age-specific theme activities

Puzzles, stackers and shape sorters

Age guide: Under 5
Aim: To enjoy using our gifts

Make available an assortment of floor puzzles, shape sorters and stackers, suitable for the age group you are working with. Encourage the children to move around the room, trying the different activities. Help them to think about their own individual gifts as they complete the activities.

At the end of the worship, place all the toys in the centre of the space and make a circle with the group around them. Offer a short prayer thanking God for all the gifts and skills used in the play activity.

Challenge game

Age guide: Under 10
Aim: To enjoy using our gifts

Set up a number of challenges around the room for children to complete. The challenges should use many different gifts that God has given us, such as our senses, our thoughts and our motor abilities, and should cater for a variety of attributes. Below are some suggested challenges, but you will be able to think of many more.

- Complete a 20-piece (maximum) jigsaw puzzle, without the picture for help.
- Identify small items on a tray covered with a cloth. Do not peek!
- Order counters or blocks into a colour (or other) sequence.
- Identify the flavour of a common food, such as crisps or dried fruit, without seeing the packaging. (Be aware of food allergies.)
- Identify a variety of scented items in pre-prepared jars or bags.

- With a hoop placed on the floor, bounce a ball inside the hoop a set number of times.
- Using a pile of connecting building pieces, build a windmill within a set time.
- Complete dot-to-dot pictures.
- Sing a chosen chorus or nursery rhyme.

Set a time limit for completing each task, such as three minutes, with a bell (or something similar) to show when it is time to move on to the next challenge. Everyone starts in a different place.

Remind the children that it is not a competition or a race, but an individual challenge. To make it more fun, each child could collect a sticker for each completed challenge.

When all the challenges are completed or the time available has run out, stop the game. Talk about the different skills and gifts needed to complete each challenge. Encourage the children to talk honestly about which challenges were easy or hard for them. Would some challenges be easier if they could use the gifts of others to help them?

Finish the worship by giving thanks to God for all the gifts we have.

Talent consequences

Age guide: Over 10
Aim: To recognise our talents

This is a game of picture consequences. Everyone has a piece of A5 plain paper and a pencil or pen at the start of the game. As the game proceeds, different parts of the body are added to form a completed outline of a person. The parts are added in the following stages.

1. Everyone draws a person's head on their paper and labels it with a gift of their own that is associated with the head, such as the brain, eyes, mouth and so on. The paper is then folded over to

hide all but the very bottom of the neck of the drawing and it is passed on to the next person. (To avoid confusion, decide in advance which way you are going to pass the papers.)

2. Without looking at what has already been drawn, everyone draws on their newly passed picture the upper part of the body, down to the waist and elbow, and labels it with a gift of their own that is associated with the heart. The paper is folded to hide what has been drawn and passed on as before.

3. Again without looking at what is already on the paper, everyone adds the lower part of the body, including the forearms and hands (but not the legs), and labels it with a gift of their own that is associated with the hands. The paper is again folded and passed on.

4. Everyone adds the legs next, labelled with a gift of their own that is associated with the legs. The paper is folded and passed on.

5. The last part of the body to be added is the feet. People label them with a gift of their own that is associated with feet. The paper is folded and passed on for the last time.

When everyone has a folded picture in their hands, they can open it up to see the full picture. Taking turns, the pictures are introduced to the group and their collective gifts are read out.

The people in the pictures will probably be comical in appearance, having been drawn by a variety of people who have not seen what was drawn before, but the gifts they represent are many and varied and very real.

Place the pictures on the floor among the group and give thanks to God for all the gifts discovered in this activity.

Sharing a meal together

People will need advance notice that the meal is going to happen, so that they can think about and prepare what they want to share.

Ask everyone to prepare a party food that they like to make. It can be as simple as crackers topped with cheese or as time-consuming as freshly made cakes. It is good if a range of foods can be made, so some coordination would be helpful. Ask people to play to their strengths: some will find it easier to make savoury nibbles and others to make desserts; some will prefer to make drinks or sweets. If everyone makes enough to share, there should be plenty of different things to try.

When all the foods are laid out on a table, encourage everyone to share the story behind the food. Did they choose to make that particular food because it is easy or perhaps because it is a family favourite? Did they make it because it reminds them of something else, or because it is a regional or cultural speciality?

If there is time, talk about the process for making the foods and ask the group, 'Does anyone think they can make everything on this table?' It would be surprising if anyone said 'Yes!' When it seems the right time in the worship to eat, enjoy the food together.

Ideas for reflection, prayer and sung worship

Reflection

Read Romans 12:4–8 and the reflection on the passage (see pp. 16–17) at the beginning of the worship.

Prayer

Thank God for all the gifts in your church. Use different voices to read out the gifts, each prayer beginning with a generic phrase. For example:

- 'Thank you, God, for the gift of singing.'
- 'Thank you, God, for the gift of organising the flower rota.'
- 'Thank you, God, for the gift of smiling.'

Hymns and songs

- Be still for the presence of the Lord (CH; JP; MP; TS)
- As we are gathered, Jesus is here (CH; MP; RS; TS)
- God it was who said to Abraham (LB)
- For I'm building a people of power (JP; MP; TS)
- Brother, sister, let me serve you (CH; RS)
- We are your people, Lord, by your grace (HAM; RS)
- There's a spirit in the air (CH; HAM; HP; RS)

Taking it further

The task activity may have brought out some new ideas. If your church agrees to embrace any of the new ideas, it will need to be taken forward by one or two members. Setting a timescale for the new idea to be implemented would probably be helpful.

Make a display for the church showing the gifts of those who worship in that place. The gifts can be shown in words, drawings, pictures or a combination of all three. At the centre of the display, place a large group photograph of the church community. Intermingled with the gifts, place the Christian names of everyone at the church. (It doesn't matter if some have the same name—just include that name as many times as it is needed.) The end result should be a large piece of wall art showing names and pictures of a variety of gifts and those who have them in the church.

NB: For reasons of child protection, do not include surnames or put children's names close to their own photographs. Check denominational guidelines for further information.

— Theme 2 —

Let the water flow

Suggested month
February

Season of the year
Winter

Christian season
Lent

Colour
Purple

Theme introduction

February brings a mixture of weather. Some days are damp and misty and others are covered in a hoar frost so deep that it lingers for several days at a time. Water is present in many forms—snow, frost, ice, rain and even steam that rises from our damp clothes when we come into warm homes. The rain can be heavy, as an old saying predicts ('February fills the dyke'), and sometimes it can be quite light. Whatever is happening in the sky above us, though, under the ground bulbs, roots and animals are beginning to stir.

February is a short month but it can feel very long. Lent begins in February, and many people help themselves to remember the season by giving something up—perhaps a luxury of some kind or a favourite food, such as chocolate.

Food is a necessity of life, as is water. Both are needed to help us live and thrive, but not all people on this earth have what they need. Water is essential not just to sustain our physical life but for many other uses, too. Water can also be destructive, however, causing damage and loss of life. This theme explores our relationship with water and looks at how both too much and too little can have an enormous impact on us and the environment in which we live.

Biblical context

Moses and Aaron went to the entrance to the sacred tent, where they bowed down. The Lord appeared to them in all his glory and said, 'Moses, get your walking stick. Then you and Aaron call the people together and command that rock to give you water. That's how you will provide water for the people of Israel and their livestock.' Moses obeyed and took his stick from the sacred tent. After he and Aaron had gathered the people around the rock, he said, 'Look, you rebellious people, and you will see water flow from this rock!' He raised his stick in the air and struck the rock two times. At once, water gushed from the rock, and the people and their livestock had water to drink.

NUMBERS 20:6–11

Reflection

Water played a big part in the life of Moses. When he was born in Egypt, there was an order in place to kill all Hebrew newborn boys. His mother kept him safe until he was three months old. She then placed him in a basket and floated it among the reeds of the River Nile, hoping that he would survive. Moses' sister watched as he was found and adopted by the Pharaoh's daughter. His sister then arranged for him to be nursed by her mother until he was old enough to live in Pharaoh's household. Moses grew up to become the leader of the Israelite people. God spoke to him, and he and his brother Aaron led the people out of Egypt, where they had been enslaved.

During the journey out of Egypt, the Israelites found their way blocked by the Red Sea. God made a path right through the sea by dividing the waters, so the people passed through with walls of water to their left and right. They reached dry land before the water was released and, when it was, it drowned the Egyptians who were pursuing them.

In the story in Numbers 20:6–11, the people of Israel were in the desert. They were hungry and thirsty, but there was no water for them or their animals. God provided water for them using Moses and a rock.

These three examples show that water saved Moses' life on many occasions: it was his hiding-place, it was his protector and it sustained and nourished his body. Water has many uses. It can be destructive and gentle, deadly and life-giving, but one thing is certain—we cannot live without it.

Theme exploration

To set the scene, have a display area draped in a purple cloth. Add something that relates to water in the world around us, such as pictures of stormy skies, an umbrella, some ice or a jug of water.

Creative discussion of water and life

In the Bible reflection, we saw what effect water had in Moses' life. In small groups of mixed ages, think about what uses water has in our lives (drinking, washing, cooking and so on) and in our churches (baptismal font, holy water for blessing, water for the minister to wash his or her hands, and so on).

Give each group a large piece of paper and some coloured pens. Ask them to draw pictures of the thoughts they produce in this activity, and make them as colourful as possible. The sheets will become a pictorial reference of ideas (a montage).

Groups might like to draw a border around the montage when it is finished, or draw a box on to the blank sheet before they start, as a space for the pictures to be drawn in. They could draw a large circle and divide it into segments to define the areas of their thoughts. Give the groups the following headings to help order their thoughts, and encourage them to be creative.

- Water in our daily lives
- Water in the places in which we live
- Water in our church
- Water in the world

Encourage the groups to think about water in both positive and negative ways. Too little water causes drought, disease and death, and too much water causes flooding, disease and destruction. Too much or too little water can cause crops to fail and drinking water supplies to become contaminated.

As the pictures are drawn, the conversation can flow freely. Some people may have questions about different aspects of water and its effects. Others will probably be able to answer the questions; if not, the group will simply have to find the answers another time.

When the groups have finished creating their sheets of water pictures, put the sheets on or near the display area. The montages will be used later in the worship.

Give it up for Lent

Lent is the period of 40 days (excluding Sundays) before Easter, and parallels the 40 days that Jesus spent in the desert at the start of his ministry (Luke 4:1–13). When Jesus was in the desert, he was tempted by the devil three times. Each time, he resisted the temptation, even though he was weak and vulnerable.

People often give up things they enjoy during the time of Lent. Some give up a favourite food, such as chocolate, as a way of denying themselves something that they like. This helps them to remember the sacrifice that Jesus made. Others give up a favourite food, save the money they would have spent on it over the period of Lent and give that money to people in need. Some deny themselves all luxuries during Lent and spend much of the time in prayer.

Water is not something that could be given up. Water is needed to sustain all life, and the human body has to have water to be able to work effectively. Sadly, for some people, there is little choice: they do not choose to give up water; they simply do not have any.

Linking the above two activities together, decide to 'give it up' and raise some money for those who have very little water. Find out about charities such as Christian Aid and Water Aid (see p. 35 for contact details), which find ways to help people with little water to help themselves.

Age-specific theme activities

Using water game

Age guide: Under 5
Aim: To think about how we use water

Have ready a number of items that are used for activities involving water. For example:

- Toothbrush: cleaning teeth
- Cup: drinking water
- Washing-up bowl and brush: doing the washing up
- Watering can: watering the plants
- Animal drinking container: looking after pets
- Soap and flannel: keeping clean
- Paintbrush and paints: making pictures

- Flour and other cooking ingredients: baking
- Vase and flowers: keeping flowers alive
- Water play toys: water games

Hide all the objects from view. Show the objects, one at a time, to the children and ask them to say how we use each one with water and for what purpose. When all the objects have been guessed, continue the worship by using as many of the items as can reasonably be used. For example, everyone could have a drink of water and then do the washing up in the bowl. Alternatively, make up a story that uses all the items. Encourage the children to point to the correct object or mime the action needed to use the object as it comes into the story. The story can be as silly as the imagination allows.

With or without water

Age guide: Under 10
Aim: To think about the difference water makes

Water is naturally present in most foods and plays different roles in them. In the case of dried fruit, the water has been removed, whereas water is added to tea leaves to enable them to infuse and become a palatable drink.

This activity shows the children examples of foods in which water makes a difference. Enjoy using the senses to see, touch, smell, taste and hear the difference it makes.

- Dried fruit versus fresh fruit: Many fruits can be bought dried or fresh. Cut fresh and dried versions of fruits (such as dates, apples or bananas) into smallish pieces and let the children taste them. What do they feel and smell like? Do the different versions taste different? What happens if the dried fruits are soaked in water? Be mindful of any allergies in the group.

31

- **Store cupboard experiment:** Provide a variety of dried ingredients that change form when water is added to them. Items such as porridge oats, sugar, couscous, cornflour, dried pasta shapes, rice, stock cubes and baking powder are all suitable. Place each one in a separate bowl or cup and ask the children to guess what is likely to happen before the water is added to each ingredient. Add warm water to them (use hot water if you are in a safe environment to do so). Demonstrate the changes that take place. Some change quickly and others take a little time. Some will swell and some will dissolve, while baking powder will gently fizz. Use as many different ingredients as desired and aim for as many different outcomes as possible. Sum up the activity by thinking about what difference water makes to us.

River of life

Age guide: Over 10
Aim: To create our own water story, similar to the story of Moses

The Bible context for this theme focuses on the story of Moses, using times in his life when water made a significant difference. There were also key moments in Jesus' life when water had great significance (for example, at his baptism and during the storm on the lake). Also, when he was tempted in the desert, water would have been his only means of survival, as the Bible tells us that he had nothing to eat during those 40 days.

Ask the group to think about their own story involving water. It might include their own baptism, a special holiday or fun times playing with water. Give each person some paper and pens and ask them to chart their own water story.

If people wish to talk about their water stories, let them do so. When the stories are completed, place them on the display table.

Sharing a meal together

The day before Lent begins is called Shrove Tuesday. Pancakes have become associated with Shrove Tuesday because they are a good way of using up rich foods such as dairy products, which, traditionally, were not eaten during the fasting period of Lent.

* Pancakes can be made in advance and reheated. A number of fillings can be made available: people will have their own traditions and favourites.
* Provide a large bowl of jelly (prepared the day before). Jelly is made using water.
* Have a variety of drinks that are made using water, such as tea, coffee, squash and so on.

Ideas for reflection, prayer and sung worship

Reflection

For many people, water is simply always there: a tap is turned and out it pours. For others, though, that is not the case: water is in short supply and is often contaminated. Moses and the people with him knew what it felt like to go without and to trust that God would provide even their simplest of needs. Water is the gift of life—this should not be forgotten. Think about what water does for you in your life.

Prayer suggestions

Make a simple water feature

Pile up some stones in the centre of a bowl and have a small jug of water ready. Keep the bowl and the jug on the display table throughout the worship. When prayers are being said, gently pour the water over the stones and let it cascade down into the bowl.

Using artwork in prayer

Place all the water montages, and any other pictures created during the worship, on the floor around the bowl of water. Place the pebbles randomly around the pictures. Invite everyone to walk around and view the pictures. If they see an image of water that inspires them to pray, either thanking God for water or asking God for help, they pick up the pebble nearest to the image, hold it in their hands and say their prayer. When they have finished their prayer, they place the pebble in the bowl of water.

When everyone has finished placing pebbles in the bowl, someone picks up the bowl and places it on the display table. Everyone says 'Amen' together.

Hymns and songs

Use any hymns or songs that focus on water, in particular the water of life.

- There's a spirit in the air (CH; HAM; HP; RS)
- Thine be the glory, risen, conquering Son (CH; MP; HAM; HP; RS; TS)
- I cannot tell why he, whom angels worship (MP; HP; RS)
- River, wash over me (MP; TS)
- Our God is so great (TS)

Taking it further

Instead of 'giving something up' for Lent, you might consider taking something up instead. Try, learn or do something that can make a difference in your life or to someone else's life.

Water Aid is an international charity that has existed since 1981. Its vision is of a world where everyone has access to safe water and sanitation. Water Aid runs various schemes, in which churches can participate, that help others who do not have access to clean running water. Find out more at www.wateraid.org.

Christian Aid is an organisation with a history going back to the end of World War II. Christian Aid believes in a world free of injustice and poverty, and helps people irrespective of their religion, nationality or ethnicity. Find out more at www.christianaid.org.uk.

*

One body, one meal, one church

Suggested month
March

Season of the year
Spring

Christian season
Holy Week

Colour
Violet (purple)

Theme introduction

March arrives with brightening skies, the days begin to grow longer again and light green buds on the trees herald the early signs of spring. Everywhere there is a sense of new beginnings, a tangible feeling of hope and thoughts of new life about to arrive but not yet here.

There is much to do all around us. In gardens, preparation is under way for a new season of growth. The plants themselves must begin to muster the energy that has lain dormant all winter and begin the long, slow journey from deep sleep back to full life. In trees, bushes, guttering and old chimneypots, birds are busy gathering ingredients to knit a new nest, preparing for the arrival of their chicks. In homes, windows are flung wide open to let the fresh air in and spring cleaning takes place to get the home ready for the rest of the year.

Holy Week is the time for Christians to prepare for the new beginning that springs into life on Easter Day. This theme looks at the days leading up to the crucifixion but focuses on the meal that Jesus shared with his friends. The theme encourages the local church to look anew at its own practice regarding the sacrament of Holy Communion and what sharing that meal means to us all as individuals as well as a church family.

Together the church is encouraged to explore how everyone can share a meal to help us remember Jesus. We can all feel the real hope of that first Easter Day. The challenge is: how can we prepare ourselves to welcome the new dawn?

Biblical context

During the meal Jesus took some bread in his hands. He blessed the bread and broke it. Then he gave it to his disciples and said, 'Take this and eat it. This is my body.' Jesus picked up a cup of wine and gave thanks to God. He gave it to his disciples and said, 'Take this and drink it. This is my blood, and with it God makes his agreement with you. It will be poured out, so that many people will have their sins forgiven. From now on I am not going to drink any wine, until I drink new wine with you in my Father's kingdom.' Then they sang a hymn and went out to the Mount of Olives.

MATTHEW 26:26–30

Jesus took some bread in his hands and gave thanks for it. He broke the bread and handed it to his apostles. Then he said, 'This is my body, which is given for you. Eat this as a way of remembering me!' After the meal he took another cup of wine in his hands. Then he said, 'This is my blood. It is poured out for you, and with it God makes his new agreement.'

LUKE 22:19–20

Reflection

The account of the meal that Jesus shared with his friends, now known as the Lord's Supper or Holy Communion, can be found in several places in the New Testament. Accounts appear in three of the Gospels and, in 1 Corinthians 11:17–34, Paul writes to the people of Corinth about the way they are sharing the Lord's Supper with each other. Paul is angry with the people because not everyone is being included at the Lord's Supper. Paul summarises the Gospel passages and reminds the people what Jesus meant when he shared the meal with his disciples. Finally, he tells them how they should share the meal with each other in remembrance of Jesus.

The meal that Jesus shared was a celebration for the festival of Passover. It was a simple meal that would have been very familiar, as it is today, to all Jewish people at the time. The fact that Jesus chose items already on the table—bread and wine—as symbols of his body and blood is significant because it shows that he wanted the symbols of remembrance to be the everyday things of life.

The mood must have been fairly jovial at first: this was a group of friends together, tired after working hard, sitting, eating and drinking together. But then the mood changed. Jesus took some bread, broke it and gave a piece to each of his disciples. In Luke's account, he asked his disciples to eat it and remember him. Taking the wine, he likened it to his own blood and talked of a new agreement between God and his people—not just the disciples but everyone, for all time. The disciples must have felt a mixture of emotions hearing Jesus' words as they shared this ordinary meal of bread and wine.

Theme exploration

To set the scene, have a display area draped with a purple cloth. Add something that relates to the world around us, such as some soil, a packet of seeds for planting, and planting tools. Include some cleaning items such as a duster or dustpan and brush. Have some bread and a bunch of grapes.

Our church is like...

With all ages working together, invite everyone to find an everyday object in the room or from their own possessions. Taking turns, each person holds the object up for everyone to see, and says: 'Our church is like... [whatever the object is] because... [whatever the reason is].' For example, 'Our church is like this chair because it is comfortable' or 'Our church is like this necklace that my mother gave me because it is very precious.'

Memorable meals

Celebrations such as birthdays, weddings, anniversaries, Christmas and Easter all involve food in some way. Whether it is an intimate dinner for two, a family meal or a party for lots of people, food will always be present and will be part of the occasion. Some foods are specifically linked with different celebrations: they might include Christmas cake, pancakes, Simnel cake, sprouts, hot cross buns, cinder toffee, mince pies, pumpkin pie, sausages on sticks and so on. Think about these foods, and add your own regional variations.

In groups of mixed ages or age-specific groups, have a discussion about memorable meals—what they included and why they were memorable. Think about celebration foods such as birthday and Christmas cakes, hot cross buns and pancakes. What do they help us to remember? Invite each group to share the salient points of their discussion with everyone.

Age-specific theme activities

Kim's game

Age guide: Under 5
Aim: To think about remembering

Have a number of easy-to-identify objects assembled on a tray. The objects could be identified by colour, shape or name, depending on the ages and abilities of the group members. The number of objects on the tray also needs to match the capability of the group.

Cover the tray and place it in front of the children. Tell everyone that they need to look carefully at the items on the tray when you remove the cloth and remember what they are, because you are going to cover them again. Remove the cloth and let the children study the tray for a minute, then cover the items again. Ask the children to hide their eyes while you remove an object from the tray. Then see if the children can guess which item is missing. Continue to play for as long as interest is sustained.

Red, blue, yellow, green

Age guide: Under 5

Allocate each of the four colours to different areas of the worship space. It could simply be that each wall, or each corner of the room, is given one of the colours. The game starts with everyone in the middle of the room. When the leader calls out a colour, the children need to move to the correct place—which means that they need to remember where each colour is positioned in the worship space. To make the game more challenging, call out items associated with a colour rather than the colour itself—for example, a poppy, the sky, a banana, grass and so on.

Learn a rhyme or song

Age guide: Under 5

Teach the group a little rhyme or song. It can be a funny rhyme or song, or one with a particular message. Some children will find this easier than others and help may be needed.

The perfect meal

Age guide: Under 10
Aim: To think about the parts of a meal and what they mean

This is an opportunity to think about the 'perfect meal' as chosen by the person creating it. There is no right or wrong way and no guidelines needed—anything goes in this meal.

Make available a number of magazines with pictures of food in them (supermarkets often give away their own magazines free) and scissors with which to cut out the pictures. Alternatively, provide coloured pens or pencils for drawings of food. Provide paper plates on which meals can be created from the pictures, or sheets of paper on which menus can be written and illustrated.

Ask everyone to choose which special meal they are going to design. Give a number of options, such as 'family Christmas dinner', 'birthday meal' or 'picnic', if that is helpful. When their choice is made, the children can create the meal or menu. As the creativity takes place, talk about what is needed for the meal, what ingredients will need to be gathered and why the children have made their particular choices. Have they taken everyone's tastes into consideration?

When everyone has finished, clear away the magazines, scissors and drawing materials, leaving the meals or menus on the table.

Have ready two paper plates, one showing the Passover meal and the other showing the elements of Holy Communion. The plates should made up in the same style as the children's creations, so that they look similar. The Passover meal plate should include pictures of:

- Matzo (unleavened bread), which is eaten three times during the meal.
- A lamb bone to represent a sacrifice. (When the temple at Jerusalem was the centre of religious life, the people went there to offer sacrifices of a lamb or a goat.)
- An egg to represent sacrifice and as an example of a food that becomes hard when cooked, symbolising the Israelites' determination not to abandon their beliefs when oppressed by the Egyptians.
- Greenery (usually lettuce) to represent new life.
- Salt water to represent a slave's tears.
- Four cups of wine to recall the four times God promised freedom to the Israelites, and to symbolise liberty and joy.
- Charoset (a paste made of apples, nuts, cinnamon and wine) to represent the mortar used by the Israelites to build the palaces of Egypt.

Talk about the Passover meal that Jesus and his friends shared together. Each item of food is a reminder of a specific event in Jewish history. Explain what each symbol meant.

Make the link with the meal that Jesus invited his friends to share with him—another remembering meal. As they had just shared the Passover meal, the symbolism of this second meal would have made a big impact on Jesus' friends.

The Lord's Supper

Age guide: Over 10
Aim: To look at how the Lord's Supper is celebrated and what the liturgy means

The leader of this activity will need to be familiar with the liturgy for Holy Communion used in your church.

Some of the group will be familiar with taking the Lord's Supper; for others this will be a new venture into the meaning and partaking of the sacrament.

Working in small groups, look at the liturgy used in your church for sharing Holy Communion. Taking it section by section, look carefully at the words and discuss what they mean. For some people this may seem like an easy task and for others it will feel hard. The point is that, through discussing it with each other, we can better understand what we say and do when we share the meal of bread and wine in Jesus' name.

Sharing a meal together

This is an opportunity to share a meal together as a community of God's people. Some advance thinking and preparation will need to take place.

The meal should be substantial but simple. It should be a main meal, prepared together and eaten together after worship. Think about who should be at the meal and make sure everyone knows that they are welcome to come and share in this time of fellowship. Choose a menu to suit the group: there may need to be choices offered.

Ensure that all those who want to do the preparation can do so. Not everyone needs to be involved in the cooking. The meal can take place only when the table has been set and everyone has been made welcome. The drinks need to be poured, and a special 'thank you' prayer (a grace) may be written. All these gifts are needed in the arrangement of the meal. As all the preparations are taking place, think about where Jesus and his friends ate their meal.

When the meal table is ready, move some bread and grapes from the display area to the centre of the dining table (leaving some behind as a visual aid for the prayers). If there are several tables, share the grapes and bread among the tables. When everyone is seated, the prayer of thanks can be said. Alternatively, everyone can sing a 'thank you' grace for the meal and then the serving can begin. Some might like to take a moment during the meal to share the bread and the grapes, remembering Jesus as they do so.

Some might like to incorporate bread and wine as part of the meal, using a suitable liturgy that will include all who wish to take the bread and wine. A discussion with parents beforehand might be advisable if young children are to be involved and it is not their usual practice to share in the bread and wine of Communion.

Ideas for reflection, prayer and sung worship

Reflection

Sharing a meal with others is a sociable and intimate thing to do. Setting aside time to enjoy the meal makes it feel special and memorable. Sharing the bread and wine together is a way of remembering Jesus and what he did for us. This meal is special and allows us to be intimate with God. When you take the bread and wine, allow your heart and soul to be in community with God.

Prayer suggestions

While people are coming together for worship, arrange for a soloist to sing the song 'As we are gathered, Jesus is here'. The singing could be accompanied by a guitar.

Pens and pieces of paper cut into the shape of vine leaves are needed for this prayer. Gather everyone around the display area or move the display to a central place so that everyone can see it. Place the grapes and the bread at the centre of the display, and place the paper vine leaves around the bread and grapes.

Suggest that everyone creates their own prayer focusing on the events of Holy Week. The prayers can be written on the paper leaves and replaced around the bread and grapes, or they can simply be spoken to God. While the prayers are being made, the soloist sings 'As we are gathered' again. He or she may need to repeat the song several times, and others can join in the singing if they wish.

Hymns and songs

Use songs and hymns that are favoured or easy to understand by all ages, such as the ones suggested below.

- As we are gathered (CH; MP; RS)
- Brother, sister, let me serve you (CH; RS)
- Dear Lord, to you again our gifts we bring (CH; HAM; RS)
- Now let us from this table rise (CH; HAM; HP; RS)
- Jesus calls us here to meet him (CH; LB)
- Let us break bread together on our knees (MP; HAM; HP; RS)
- An upper room did our Lord prepare (HAM; HP; RS)

Taking it further

Hold a Tenebrae service during Holy Week. Tenebrae (a Latin word meaning 'darkness') is a service of readings that takes place on one or all of the last three evenings before Easter Day, depending on your tradition. One candle is lit for each of the readings. In some traditions there are nine candles and readings; in others there are 15.

The office of Tenebrae is a reflective and sombre service that dates back to medieval times and reminds us why the crucifixion took place—so that our sins could be forgiven. It is a powerful service, so it is helpful to give an explanation to young people before they take part.

A small gathering might hold the service around tables placed in the shape of a cross, on which candles are positioned and lit. In a larger gathering, the candles can be placed around the church or together at the front for all to see.

The service can start with a gentle hymn but, as it progresses, music and sound are kept to a minimum. After each reading has been read, one candle is extinguished so that the light is gradually banished from the room, leaving people sitting silently in darkness. A loud noise, such as a book being closed, a door slamming or the clashing of a symbol, symbolising Jesus' death, signals the end of the worship. Everyone leaves in darkness and silence.

The history of the Tenebrae service and liturgies to conduct the service on Maundy Thursday or Good Friday are available in some worship books and on the internet. Printed below is a short version of a service of Tenebrae. You can add poems or reflections to this outline and, if the service is to be held on Maundy Thursday, share Holy Communion together as part of the worship (but before the office of Tenebrae begins).

The service should be conducted meditatively and without announcement, and there should be one minute's silence between each reading. The electric lights in the room or church should be dimmed and the candles already lit for the start of the service. Have some background music playing as people arrive and sit down.

For the service you will need a leader, ten readers, nine candles (or tealight candles) and a special candle to represent Jesus (the Christ candle).

Leader: Jesus sets out on his final journey to Jerusalem. The cross is ahead of him, overshadowing the miracles he performed and the hope that his teachings brought. The disciples do not yet understand the true nature of his calling and sacrifice. They do not know of what he is talking when he speaks of betrayal and promise, spilt blood and a broken body. Let us read and remember.

Reader 1:   *(Reads Luke 18:31–34)*

Extinguish a candle.

Reader 2:   Jesus came to Jerusalem. He said to the disciples…
            (Reads John 12:35–36)

No candle is blown out.

Reader 3:   It was the time of Passover. Jesus and the disciples
            were gathered together to share the meal. *(Reads
            Matthew 26:20–25)*

Extinguish a candle.

Reader 4:   *(Reads Matthew 26:31–35)*

Extinguish a candle.

Reader 5:   Accompanied by the disciples, Jesus went to the
            Mount of Olives. *(Reads Mark 14:32–41)*

Extinguish a candle.

Reader 6:   *(Reads Matthew 26:47–52)*

Extinguish a candle.

Reader 7:   *(Reads Luke 22:54–62)*

Extinguish a candle.

Reader 8:   Jesus was taken before Pilate. (*Reads John 18:33–38*)

Extinguish a candle.

Reader 9:   A large crowd had gathered. Jesus was brought
             before them. (*Reads Matthew 27:20–26*)

Extinguish a candle.

Reader 10: (*Reads Mark 15:16–20*)

Extinguish a candle.

Leader: (*Reads John 19:30b*)

*The final candle, the Christ candle, is extinguished. Everyone sits
in darkness and silence.*

Have minimal lighting so that people can see well enough to leave
in silence. There is no closing prayer.
    Light the Christ candle again on Easter morning.

*

Celebrate life

Suggested month
April

Season of the year
Spring

Christian season
Easter

Colour
White or gold

Theme introduction

This month is known for its 'April showers' but there are often chilly days and warm days along with the sudden outbursts of rain. Around about us, spring flowers are beginning to pop up, adding colour to window boxes, gardens and town centres. Trees have a bright yellowy green hue and the woodlands carry the purple haze of bluebells.

New life is everywhere, using its strength to push through the ground, fight off the winter hibernation and emerge victorious where death seemed all-dominant.

In the Christian context, this is exactly what we see happening as we look again at the amazing details that surround the Easter story. The challenge of Jesus' death and resurrection is so powerful and so humbling that, as Christians, we stand in awe of the reality of what that new life means to us.

This theme encourages everyone to look at different parts of the story, to think about why events unfolded in the way they did, and to have a better understanding of the story itself. The church embarks on a familiar journey, revisiting favourite places in this narrative but coming face-to-face with the challenge that confronts each of us when we realise the significance of what Jesus did for us.

Biblical context

The reflection on these passages will take place as part of the 'Theme exploration'.

About midday the sky turned dark and stayed that way until around three o'clock. Then about that time Jesus shouted, 'Eloi, Eloi, lema sabachthani?' which means, 'My God, my God, why have you deserted me?' Some of the people standing there heard Jesus and said, 'He is calling for Elijah.' One of them ran and grabbed a sponge. After he had soaked it in wine, he put it on a stick and held it up to Jesus. He said, 'Let's wait and see if Elijah will come and take him down!' Jesus shouted and then died. At once the curtain in the temple tore in two from top to bottom. A Roman army officer was standing in front of Jesus. When the officer saw how Jesus died, he said, 'This man really was the Son of God!'

MARK 15:33–39

After the Sabbath, Mary Magdalene, Salome, and Mary the mother of James bought some spices to put on Jesus' body. Very early on Sunday morning, just as the sun was coming up, they went to the tomb. On their way, they were asking one another, 'Who will roll the stone away from the entrance for us?' But when they looked, they saw that the stone had already been rolled away. And it was a huge stone! The women went into the tomb, and on the right side they saw a young man in a white robe sitting there. They were alarmed. The man said, 'Don't be alarmed! You are looking for Jesus from Nazareth, who was nailed to a cross. God has raised him to life, and he isn't here. You can see the place where they put his body. Now go and tell his disciples, and especially Peter, that he will go ahead of you to Galilee. You will see him there, just as he told you.' When the women ran from the tomb, they were confused and shaking all over. They were too afraid to tell anyone what had happened.

MARK 16:1–8

While Jesus' disciples were talking about what had happened, Jesus appeared and greeted them. They were frightened and terrified because they thought they were seeing a ghost. But Jesus said, 'Why are you so frightened? Why do you doubt? Look at my hands and my feet and see who I am! Touch me and find out for yourselves. Ghosts don't have flesh and bones as you see I have.' After Jesus said this, he showed them his hands and his feet. The disciples were so glad and amazed that they could not believe it. Jesus then asked them, 'Do you have something to eat?' They gave him a piece of baked fish. He took it and ate it as they watched.

Jesus said to them, 'While I was still with you, I told you that everything written about me in the Law of Moses, the Books of the Prophets, and in the Psalms had to happen.' Then he helped them understand the Scriptures. He told them: The Scriptures say that the Messiah must suffer, then three days later he will rise from death. They also say that all people of every nation must be told in my name to turn to God, in order to be forgiven. So beginning in Jerusalem, you must tell everything that has happened. I will send you the one my Father has promised, but you must stay in the city until you are given power from heaven.

LUKE 24:36–49

Theme exploration

To set the scene, have a display area draped with a white or gold cloth. Add something that relates to the world around us, perhaps a young plant in a pot, some new leaves from a tree or some pictures showing new life.

Discovering the story

There are numerous themes that emerge with the story of Easter, such as betrayal, fear, hope, communion, disbelief, resurrection and new life. Many of them weave in and out of several parts of the story. The three Bible passages chosen for this theme focus on Jesus' death and resurrection, but, if time allows, more of the story could be explored.

Divide into three groups. Each group takes one of the Bible readings and is given ten minutes to talk about the passage and what it means to them. Be mindful that death is a difficult subject for some people to talk about, especially if they have been bereaved or if they are very young.

When each group has discussed its passage, share the story with each other. The passages do not need to be read, just told as a story. Explanations can be given for parts of the story if they are needed.

The group with Mark 15:33–39 should begin, followed by the group with Mark 16:1–8 and, finally, the group with Luke 24:36–49.

Reflection

These three passages tell the story of how Jesus' death and resurrection affected those who witnessed the events as they happened.

The first passage is a painful one to encounter. It describes the actual moment of Jesus' death. Anyone who has experienced the death of a loved one will understand the pain felt by those who knew Jesus as a son or friend, as they watched his unjust death. The scene was dramatic: the sky turned dark, people were shocked and saddened by recent events and Jesus cried out to God in his pain, 'Why have you deserted me?' in the same way that a child calls for help when he or she has been hurt. This is a moment when Jesus seems unmistakably human, and yet he addresses his Father as 'my God', showing, even at the moment of death, his respect and humility.

The impact of the passage is softened for readers today by the knowledge of what happened next and the reality of the resurrection.

The second passage shows us the reactions of those close to Jesus. When the women visit his tomb, they are alarmed by a young man—some Gospel writers tell us that he was an angel—who shows them the empty space where Jesus had been laid. They listen as he gives them a message to tell to the other disciples, and then they run from the tomb. The grieving women are so scared and confused that they tell no one about what they have seen and heard.

The third reading gives us a glimpse of the resurrected Jesus in the midst of his friends. Having broken bread with two of his disciples in Emmaus, he now joins the wider group as the Emmaus story is being retold. He provides them with the evidence they have been searching for as he shows them his wounds. He eats with them to show that his body is real and not that of a ghost. Jesus sits among them as a friend and teacher, explaining the scriptures to them.

In hearing the accounts in these readings, we feel the hope that Jesus' death brought. With Jesus' resurrection and the empty cross, all are saved.

Age-specific theme activities

Biscuit celebrations

Age guide: Under 5
Aim: To celebrate new hope

Either buy some plain biscuits, such as Rich Tea, or make some cross-shaped biscuits using a basic biscuit recipe from a recipe book or from the internet.

Make royal icing or butter cream and have it ready for when the children arrive. Provide a variety of decorative items such as small sweets, mini eggs and sprinkles for the children to use to decorate their biscuits. Be mindful of any food allergies in the group.

Gather the children around a table or several tables. Give each child a paper plate on which their name is written. Give each of them a biscuit and help them to use the icing to cover the surface of the biscuit. Place the decorating sweets and sprinkles in the centre of the table or tables and ask the children to decorate their biscuits as you tell them a story.

Share the story of the first Easter Day with the group and tell the children that the biscuits they are making are to help them celebrate the good news. There are many excellent books that tell the Easter story in a way that is easy for children to understand. Better still, read the story yourself beforehand and then tell it to the children in your own words.

A time to dance

Age guide: Under 10
Aim: To celebrate new hope with a lively, colourful song

Have a number of instruments available or make some new ones with the group. Bring party blowers, whistles and other noisy toys to add to the instruments. Make pieces of lightweight fabric, in different colours, available for children to hold and wave around in time with the music. Alternatively, attach lengths of thin coloured ribbon or wool to newly purchased elastic hairbands.

This activity can be carried out by the children during the worship or beforehand, if desired. Decorated hairbands can be worn around the wrists as the instruments are played to enhance and encourage movement.

Choose a song or chorus that is known or can easily be taught, such as a contemporary arrangement of 'Lord of the Dance'. Sing the song a couple of times without the instruments until the children are comfortable with their singing. Share the story about Easter and explain that one way we can celebrate the good news is to make a loud and joyful noise. Give out the decorated bands or lightweight fabric and the musical instruments, then sing the song through while everyone enjoys celebrating.

A twig cross of celebration

Age guide: Over 10
Aim: To reflect on the good news of the empty cross

Plan ahead

In the week before the worship, ask children to bring some flowers and greenery from their gardens if they can. (Remind them to ask before picking and not to pull up flowers by the roots.) Bring extra flowers and greenery yourself so that everyone can participate.

Bring to the worship some string and some twigs gathered from gardens or woodlands to make a cross. If this activity is being done with young people or adults, ask them to bring twigs from their own gardens, to personalise the making of the cross. Alternatively, using chalk, draw the image of a cross on the floor of the room in which you are meeting. The flowers brought by the children will be attached to the cross or placed on the floor cross as the activity proceeds.

Making a twig cross

Gather your twigs into two bundles. Each bundle can be lengthened as required by overlapping or layering the twigs, but care will need to be taken to ensure that it holds its shape. Secure each bundle separately, then lash them together to make a cross shape, using string or other strong binding.

When the twigs are tied, add more string to the cross to allow the flowers and greenery to be slipped under it later. This string should be a little looser than that used to bind the twigs together. Some groups will be able to create the cross without help, but others may need assistance. If moss is available and can be incorporated into the cross shape, this will help the flowers and greenery to stay fresh for longer.

Place the bare cross on the floor and stand as a group around it. (Alternatively, stand around the chalked cross on the floor.) Look at the cross and how bare it is. Lying there on the floor, it is a symbol of death.

Read a suitable Bible passage, poem or verse of a hymn, talking about the time after Jesus' death when he lay in the tomb. Walk around the cross. Then encourage everyone to bring their flowers and greenery to the cross and attach them. As this is happening, present a second reading, telling of the good news that Jesus is risen.

When the cross has been decorated, invite everyone to stand back and look at it—now a vibrant symbol of new life. To close the activity, sing a triumphant hymn (see suggestions below).

Sharing a meal together

Have a social time with drinks, and share sugared Easter biscuits made by members of the church family.

Ideas for reflection, prayer and sung worship

Reflection

Having begun worship with the historic account of Jesus' death, we find ourselves with the living hope that his resurrection brings. Use the display area or the twig cross of celebration as a focal point. Read a short meditation from an Easter anthology to encourage people in their reflection.

Prayer suggestions

There are lots of anthologies of prayers and many will include sections on Easter.

Write prayers to include the key parts of the Easter story, focusing on the good news of Easter Day. Intersperse your prayers with a gentle sung chorus.

Hymns and songs

- Lord of the dance (CH; JP; HAM; RS)
- Christ the Lord is risen today (CH; MP; HAM; HP; RS)
- Alleluia, alleluia, give thanks to the risen Lord (JP; MP; HP; RS; TS)
- Led like a lamb to the slaughter (JP; MP; RS; TS)
- From heav'n you came, helpless babe (CH; JP; MP; RS; TS)
- To God be the glory (CH; MP; HP; RS; TS)
- Low in the grave he lay (JP; MP; HP; TS)

Taking it further

Use the three Bible passages as the basis for a Bible study. In small groups of three or four, spend half an hour reading and discussing all three Bible passages. Ask groups to think about the experience from the point of view of:

- The Roman army officer
- The women who went to the tomb
- The disciples when Jesus appeared to them for the first time

Ask the group to say which character they identify with. Following the discussion, share thoughts among the whole group.

Patchwork stories

Suggested month
May

Season of the year
Spring

Christian season
Ascension

Colour
White or gold

Theme introduction

May is the month when the last signs of spring give way to the early signs of summer. Wild flowers are blooming at the sides of roads and in the hedgerows, blossom falls from the trees like a cascade of confetti and the grass begins to grow with new vigour. The days feel noticeably longer and there is a new energy within many of us as well as in the natural world around us.

From the sky, the country looks amazing—a patchwork of colour and life, telling a story of the land and its people below. Fields are a mixture of colours—the yellow of oilseed rape, the brown of the earth with newly sown crops or the pink of fruit tree blossoms. In other areas, rocks are grey against the bright skies, and trees are full of bright green leaves. In the towns, the streets and buildings are 'sweet and clean now after the rains', to quote Jeff Wayne's lyrics for *War of the Worlds* (on the track 'Brave new world'), and sunlight bounces off the windows, creating giant mirrors to light the world around.

Patchwork has often been connected with storytelling. In the United Kingdom, patchwork was traditionally produced mostly as a cottage industry, and was both ornamental and utilitarian. Groups of women would gather together and piece the fabrics in place. In the home, the story was in the fabrics—remnants saved from garments no longer worn but still carrying memories. In some parts of North America, patchwork quilts are made as wedding gifts, sewn by groups in the community who tell their stories as they sew. The stories are recorded and passed on with the quilt.

Quilts have been used for passing messages as well as stories. The Underground Railroad was an informal network of routes and safe houses used to help slaves escape to freedom in America in the 19th century. Patchwork quilts were hung in visible places, such as out of windows or on fences, as if they were simply airing; but different patterns carried different meanings and, depending on the arrangement of the patterns, a message could be read. It is claimed that up to 100,000 people escaped enslavement in this way.

Through different activities, this theme looks at the church—a place full of vibrant, colourful people, living their lives as the family of God. Retelling and recording our stories, remembering shared times that were both good and challenging, is not simply about looking to the past; it enables us to think about the future together.

Biblical context

My friends, I beg you to listen as I teach. I will give instruction and explain the mystery of what happened long ago. These are things we learned from our ancestors, and we will tell them to the next generation. We won't keep secret the glorious deeds and the mighty miracles of the Lord. God gave his Law to Jacob's descendants, the people of Israel. And he told our ancestors to teach their children, so that each new generation would know his Law and tell it to the next. Then they would trust God and obey his teachings, without forgetting anything God had done.

PSALM 78:1–7

Reflection

Transmitting the history of communities and recording wise words to pass on to future generations has, throughout history, been achieved through the oral tradition. In some communities, people were set aside from other tasks to enable them to concentrate on the retelling of the stories of their people. They were respected and honoured and everyone listened when they spoke.

The psalmist clearly has something to say, some wise words to pass on, and there is an urgency with which he calls the people to listen to him. He talks of the importance of handing on to the next generation the story of the 'great deeds' that God has done. He goes on to explain that only when the story is passed from one generation to another will future generations fully understand how to live a God-centred life.

Jesus was the greatest of storytellers. He probably grew up listening to stories, and in his teaching he used stories in many different ways. He told stories to explain the scriptures, to help people to understand the message he brought and to help people to understand themselves and those around them better.

Telling stories and parables and recording the story for the future is part of our own tradition, in our families, communities and churches. The evidence of such storytelling is all around us, being told by word of mouth, in books and through objects such as wall plaques. All these means of communication tell our stories to the next generation.

Theme exploration

To set the scene, have a display area draped with a white or gold cloth. Add something that relates to the world around us, such as several pictures of fields of crops, or small newly grown plants—the more vibrant the colours, the better. Include objects in different colours, and perhaps some storybooks.

Ice breaker

Sit or stand in a big circle, or in smaller mixed-age groups if there are more than 20 people. Give everyone a moment to think of something about themselves that they are happy to tell others, which other people in the room are unlikely to know about them. When everyone has thought of something, start the game. Each person takes a turn to say his or her name and to tell the thing that others don't know about them.

Age-specific theme activities

Matching stories

Age guide: Under 5
Aim: To see how pieces of a picture come together to tell a story

Using old picture books that are no longer needed, or adverts in magazines, gather images, each of which seems to tell a story. At least one picture—of about A4 size—will be needed for each participant. If you are using magazine pictures, stick them on to card to strengthen them.

It helps if each picture is in a distinctive colour, so that they can be easily identified. If not, mount each picture on to a different coloured piece of backing card, bigger than the picture itself.

Cut each picture into four or five pieces. If they are mounted on to different coloured backing cards, make sure there is a piece of border on each of the cut shapes. Each picture will now be a mini-jigsaw with four or five pieces.

Keep one piece of each picture separate from the rest. Either place the remaining pieces around the room or mix them all up in a pile on the floor. Give each child one of the pieces that you held to one side, and ask them to find the rest of their picture.

When everyone has found their pieces, they can put together their picture and then tell the story of what they can see in it. Ask each child to share his or her story with others.

Picture it

Age guide: Under 5
Aim: To create pictures of a Bible story

Plan ahead

Beforehand, choose a Bible story to share with the group (the more familiar, the better). The story is to be told and then interpreted into pictures by the children. The pictures can be made with felt shapes and characters stuck on to a base fabric, or by using foam shapes and characters stuck on to card. It would be helpful to provide some pre-cut shapes that relate to the story (such as animals for the story of Noah). Use different coloured fabric or card for the picture bases.

Making the pictures

Tell the story, then lay out the craft equipment and encourage the children to make pictures of the story. Be ready to help when necessary, but be careful not to stifle creativity. The pictures are to be used in the worship and could be placed on a wall in the worship area, so some children might like to make a second picture to take home.

When the story pictures are completed, gather them at the display area and use them as part of worship. If the picture bases are made of fabric, they can be stitched together to make a wall-hanging (see below for more instructions). If they are made of card, they can be arranged directly on to the wall.

Memory boxes

Age guide: Under 10
Aim: To make something special to keep our own stories in

This activity enables the children to make boxes in which they can store items that have a significant meaning in their lives—a bit like a scrapbook in a box. Items might include pictures, postcards, photographs, ribbon from a present, a key ring, a sweet wrapper, a found treasure such as a shell and so on—in fact, anything that means something to them. Boxes can be bought relatively cheaply but they can just as easily be made. An ideal box would be one with a lid, such as a shoebox, but boxes without lids can also work well.

If your boxes are already decorated on the outside, carefully ease the glued 'seams' apart. When all of the seams are released, re-stick them inside out so that the plain, non-decorated inside of the box is now on the outside. This gives a clear matt surface to the box, on which to start your own decorations.

Tell the children about scrapbooks and explain that they will be making a scrapbook in a box. Tell them that the boxes can be used for a very long time, until they are full, and then another one can be started.

Provide an assortment of craft materials, coloured pencils and glue sticks, and encourage the children to make the boxes special to them. Decorate the lid first: let the children write their names on the lids, along with something that says what the box is for. If your boxes do not have lids, children could write their names on one side. Different levels of help will be needed, depending on the abilities of those in the group.

The children can take their boxes home and start collecting things in them. As time goes by, the boxes will contain a collection of items that help to tell a part of the children's own stories.

Group memory box

Age guide: Under 10
Aim: To make something special to keep our group stories in

Children might like to make a group memory box in which to collect items that relate to them as a community. As the box fills, it can be used in prayer or as a way of remembering fun times shared by the group and friends who have left.

Nature collages

Age guide: Under 10
Aim: To show the story of our surroundings

Plan ahead

Tell the group in advance that they need to bring in items from the natural world for this activity. Items could include flowers (remind the children not to pull up flowers by the root), grass, leaves, vegetable peelings, moss, feathers, tree bark, sand, weeds and so on. Bring a selection of these objects yourself for those who have come without their own.

Make the collage

Collect all the items together in one place and ask the children to sort them into an order chosen by the group. The order could be by colour, texture, size or shape. Talk about the items and their role in the natural world as they are sorted.

Use PVA glue to stick the objects, in their chosen groups, on to pieces of card. Match the card colour to colour groups, if that is how the items have been sorted. Ensure that all the items are well fixed and then leave to dry.

When the pictures have dried completely, arrange them in a colourful way to enhance the images they show. Set a border around the collage and mount it on a wall to display the wonderful story of creation that surrounds us in our everyday lives.

Our story wall-hanging

Age guide: Over 10 (also suitable for mixed ages)
Aim: Telling the story of our church

Plan ahead

This activity involves making a wall-hanging of considerable size to depict the life of your church. One or two people who can sew and have access to sewing machines will need to finish the work. Patchwork quilts are made by piecing patchwork or appliquéd blocks together. There are many block patterns and most are distinctive to the countries in which they originated. The number of blocks required depends on the desired size of the finished quilt. Blocks are worked separately and sewn together when they are completed, to make a quilt top, which is then backed. The wall-hanging will be made using the same techniques.

Several weeks before the activity is planned to take place, put a box in a prominent place and ask people to donate pieces of fabric they have cut from discarded clothes. Ask that no actual clothes are placed in the box, just unwanted fabric pieces; new fabrics could also be donated. Provide a smaller box in which people can place any rescued buttons or decorative items such as ribbons, charms, pompoms and beads.

A total of 56 blocks, each 30cm square, will be needed to complete this wall-hanging. With a border to frame the block work, the finished wall-hanging will be roughly 240cm x 214cm and can be made to hang either 'portrait' or 'landscape' style, depending on the space available.

Getting started

Divide into small groups to decide what information, events and happenings best reflect the life and story of your church. Some groups can focus on the past and some on the present. Favourite Bible stories or images from the Bible may be included, along with images from the community around the church. The decision is entirely that of the whole group.

When the groups have decided what needs to be depicted on the wall-hanging, an image needs to be allocated to each of the 56 blocks. Groups can work on different blocks together; some blocks could be taken away and worked by individuals at home or with each other in several homes.

Decide on the base colour or colours and cut out the 30cm squares, allowing 2cm all the way round as a seam allowance. The decorative work on each individual block can be done with stitching or with glue (as the finished piece will be a wall-hanging, the individual blocks will have very little wear and tear). The finished blocks will be stitched together using a sewing machine (see below) to give the whole piece strength.

Working a block

Start with the block base and lay it flat on a table. First, design on paper the image to be depicted on the block; then gather the relevant fabric pieces. The pieces need to be cut into shape and either sewn on to the block base or glued on, using PVA or fabric glue. Add any extra items, such as buttons or beads, that are needed for detail. It may be helpful to play some upbeat music, such as songs from *Joseph and his Amazing Technicolor Dreamcoat*, while the groups work.

When all the blocks are completed (this could take several weeks), lay them out on the floor to make a rectangle of 8 x 7 blocks, and play with the design until everyone is happy with the overall layout. This may involve switching blocks around a few times until they find their natural place in the flow of ideas. Take photographs of the layout for future reference. Sew the blocks into strips, and then sew the strips together. Use a sewing machine for this final stage, as this will make the block seams stronger and ensure that the hanging can take its own weight.

Cut 20cm-wide strips of fabric to create a border around the block work. Using a 2cm seam allowance again, attach the border to the longer edges first and then the shorter edges. Hem the border.

Make enough 10cm-wide hanging tabs to take the weight of the patchwork and add them to the top of the work. Finish the wall-hanging by backing it with a neutral fabric. If time and skills permit, the patchwork top can be backed with wadding and quilted (see any book on patchwork for more detailed instructions).

Only when the hanging is finally completed, and all the blocks are shown together like a giant storyboard, will the true beauty and story of your church emerge.

See page 154 for a diagram of the individual blocks and the finished wall hanging.

Sharing a meal together

Have a buffet lunch—which is similar to a patchwork, in that it is made up of different colours and textures and is provided using the many different gifts that people have. Furthermore, ultimately it is for the benefit and enjoyment of others. During the weeks before the lunch is to take place, display two lists (savoury and sweet) and ask people to sign up for the food they will bring. The lunch could be part of a day spent working on the wall-hanging.

Ideas for reflection, prayer and sung worship

Reflection

The recording and passing on of stories is a great tradition and part of our heritage. The creation of a story wall-hanging for your church will record a part of the church's own history. Its presence will be a colourful and lasting reminder (for current and future worshippers) of the vibrant, ongoing story of the people in the church.

Before the hanging is positioned in its permanent home, lay it out for everyone to see. Encourage people to walk around the hanging and 'read' the stories they see in the pictures. Some of those stories will have been intended by the makers, and others will just emerge from what is seen. Encourage people to sit by the hanging and to touch it, to feel its textures.

Read Psalm 78:1–7 and allow the words to fill the air as people reflect on the hanging and its stories.

Prayer suggestions

Write prayers for the people in your church of yesterday, today and tomorrow.

Hymns and songs

- All over the world (JS; MP)
- One more step along the world I go (CH; JP; HP; RS)
- Moses, I know you're the man (HP; RS)
- The church is like a table (RS)
- Seek ye first the kingdom of God (CH; JP; MP; HP; RS)
- Take my life, and let it be (CH; MP; HAM; HP; RS)

Taking it further

- Read Deuteronomy 6:4–9. The beginning of this passage is known in the Jewish faith as the *Shema* (from the Hebrew word meaning 'hear'). The teaching that there is only one God (not a multitude, as was commonly believed in Old Testament times) and the command to love God with the whole of our being are the basis for the majority of Jewish religious practices. Discuss the importance of this passage in the context of sharing the stories of your church.
- Share the story in the community. Tell your local newspapers about the hanging, invite them to take a photograph of it or send them one of your own photographs. Could the hanging be displayed in the library or town hall? Could it be taken to schools in the community or visit other churches? Maybe they could tell their stories too.
- Find out more about the Underground Railroad. The blocks used in the quilts that were made to help slaves to freedom each had a distinctive message and formed part of a code. Blocks sewn into the finished quilt were placed in a particular order to enable them to be read by those who knew the code.

— Theme 6 —

Beautiful prayer

Suggested month
June

Season of the year
Summer

Christian season
Pentecost

Colour
Red

Theme introduction

June is a month of long evenings and beautiful sunsets. The leaves on the trees are still fresh and green, untouched by the dust of hot summer days still to come. Our gardens, window boxes and town displays are bursting with early summer flowers and the scent of roses hangs in the air. The hedgerow is busy and elderflower fills the woodland trees. All around us there is beauty and gracefulness as creation comes into its own.

There is so much to thank God for, so many gifts. However, saying 'thank you' is only part of our conversation with God. We should be saying other things, too, such as asking for help, saying 'sorry' and praising God. Conversation is a two-way process, so we should also be listening. What does God want to say to us? What does God want us to do? How can we respond? All this can be done through prayer.

For many people both inside and outside our churches, including young people, children and new worshippers, prayer is often hard to understand. Sometimes people are anxious that they are 'just not doing it right'. Church leaders often choose not to look at the prayer life of the worshipping community, simply assuming that everyone understands prayer and knows how to communicate with God through prayer. This was the case even in Jesus' time.

This theme looks at what prayer is and how we can participate in collective and personal prayer. There is a focus on the Lord's Prayer, encouraging people to think about and understand what we are saying when we pray this prayer, both publicly and privately.

Exploring prayer in this way as a group of Christians—all at different stages of the Christian journey—will help to increase confidence in prayer. It will enable many people to realise that God does not judge us by the quality and correctness of our prayer, but simply wants to be in conversation with us.

Biblical context

Jesus continued: When you pray, don't be like those show-offs who love to stand up and pray in the meeting places and on the street corners. They do this just to look good. I can assure you that they already have their reward. When you pray, go into a room alone and close the door. Pray to your Father in private. He knows what is done in private, and he will reward you. When you pray, don't talk on and on as people do who don't know God. They think God likes to hear long prayers. Don't be like them. Your Father knows what you need before you ask. You should pray like this:

Our Father in heaven, help us to honour your name. Come and set up your kingdom, so that everyone on earth will obey you, as you are obeyed in heaven. Give us our food for today.

Forgive us for doing wrong, as we forgive others. Keep us from being tempted and protect us from evil.

If you forgive others for the wrongs they do to you, your Father in heaven will forgive you. But if you don't forgive others, your Father will not forgive your sins.

MATTHEW 6:5–15

Reflection

Jesus was talking to a crowd of people, who had followed him to the mountainside because they had heard of his teaching and the miracles he was performing. He told them how they should live their lives and explained to them what the scriptures meant, before beginning to tell them how to pray.

In his words to the crowd, Jesus tells people not to show off publically when they pray. (Some Bible translations say, 'Do not be like hypocrites.') He tells them to find a private space, a space where they can be alone with God, because prayer is a personal relationship with God. Jesus tells them how to address God and what they should remember to ask and thank God for. Then he gives them an example, saying a prayer to God that mentions all the things he has spoken about.

Jesus finishes this part of his talk by reminding his listeners that, in asking for forgiveness from God, they themselves must forgive others.

Theme exploration

To set the scene, have a display area draped with a red cloth. Add something that relates to the world around us, such as some fresh flowers, a picture of a sunset and some favourite prayers. Place a Bible in the display area, open at Matthew 6:5–15. Add books on prayers and graces to the area or write out some prayers.

On large, thin pieces of card, write sentences from the Lord's Prayer and place the cards around the room (they do not have to be in sequence). Different-coloured pieces of card will make the display look vibrant. Several sets could be written and placed around the walls. Everyone will be surrounded by the Lord's Prayer as they focus on today's theme.

Ice-breaker

Prayer is all about talking and listening to God. This ice-breaker helps us to talk and listen to each other.

With all ages together, everyone turns to a neighbour and greets him or her. They tell each other their names and how they travelled to church that day. People will need to negotiate who speaks first and who listens. Then everyone turns to another neighbour and does the same. Now we have greeted each other, used our voices and listened to our neighbours.

Prayer discussion

This activity is suitable for all ages working together in small groups. Pens and large pieces of paper, such as flipchart paper or lining wallpaper (not ready-pasted), will be needed.

Not everyone is comfortable about prayer. Some people worry about whether they are praying correctly or if God is listening to them; some worry that they are not worthy and others worry that they simply do not have the right words to address God. Talking about prayer objectively rather than emotionally will help everyone to further their own thinking.

Talk through the following questions. (The question 'Why?' will be addressed in a separate activity.) NB: Because it is important that all who participate in this discussion feel comfortable, it is not necessary to share personal practice but rather to think more in general terms.

- What is prayer?
- Who can pray?
- Where should we pray?
- How should we pray?
- When should we pray?

Each group draws a large circle on a sheet of paper and divides the circle into six segments, labelling them Who? What? Where? When? How? and Why? Invite people to write their thoughts about prayer (using the previous discussion for guidance) in the relevant segment. The 'Why?' segment should remain empty.

When each group has written all their ideas in the segments, the groups can join up in pairs and share their thinking. Mark on the segments where there are overlaps in people's thinking. If time allows, the groups can move one more time to share their answers with another group. Once again, mark on the segments where answers have been the same or similar.

Why should we pray?

Prayer generally falls into the following categories:

- Adoration: expressing our love for God
- Confession: saying 'sorry' to God for the things we have done wrong
- Thanksgiving: saying 'thank you' to God for all that is done for us
- Intercession: asking God to help others in different parts of the world
- Petition: talking to God about concerns that are particular to us

Work in small groups once more and discuss the reasons why we pray. Collect the responses in the unfilled segment of the circle.

Refer back to the segmented circle and spend a few moments simply thinking about prayer.

Remind people that by saying 'Amen' at the end of a prayer, we are saying 'I agree' or 'May it be so' to what has been said.

Age-specific theme activities

Colour speak

Age guide: Under 5
Aim: To hear our own voices and say 'thank you' to God

Invite everyone to sit in a circle. Each person is to say his or her name and a favourite colour. Start with a leader to give an example.

When everyone has had a go, have a mini treasure hunt and gather things that show all the colours chosen. Depending on the resources available, it might be necessary to bring a number of different-coloured items to the worship and place them around the room for the children to find.

When all the items are gathered together, talk about how God made everything, even the colours, and then ask the children to look at all the colours. Thank God for all the colours that can be seen and invite the children to say a loud 'thank you', too.

Prayer bookmarks

Age guide: Under 10
Aim: To make a prayer

This is a confidence-growing activity that uses craft as a means of creating a space for a conversation about prayer.

Using the ideas from the prayer discussion above, talk to the children about prayer and decide what kind of prayer they would like to show on their bookmarks. Focus on one or two kinds of prayer, such as 'please', 'thank you' or 'sorry' prayers.

Have some card available, cut into bookmark sizes, as well as some coloured pens and sticky shapes. This will be quite a detailed piece of work for some children and help may be needed.

Working in small groups so that conversation can flow easily, talk about what the children's prayers will be and write or draw them in rough on scrap paper. The prayers should be quite general so that they can be used on more than one occasion. When each child is happy with his or her prayer, it can be transferred, either by writing or drawing, on to the bookmark.

Decorate the bookmarks and cover them with clear adhesive plastic to protect them.

Prayer tree

Age guide: Under 10
Aim: To create a space where private prayers can be made

Tie together some substantial branches and 'plant' them in a large pot to resemble a tree. Make sure the pot and the 'tree' are stable. Place the tree by the display area. Place two baskets beneath the tree, one containing pegs and the other containing pieces of coloured paper and pencils. If anyone wishes to write or draw a prayer, they can use the coloured paper and peg their prayer on to the tree.

At the end of the worship, the group can gather around the prayer tree and the leader can simply offer the prayers to God. The individual prayers should not be read out, because they are private between the person concerned and God. Everyone can say 'Amen' after the leader has drawn the worship time together with a concluding prayer.

Prayer guidelines for private prayer

Age guide: Over 10
Aim: To use the ideas from the prayer discussion or any of the above activities to begin talking about prayer

The guidelines below are offered to help those beginning to experience personal prayer. They are simply guidelines and not rules. Some groups may wish to create their own.

- Praying is like having a conversation with God.
- Prayer can be done when you are in a group or when you are on your own.
- A prayer is personal and does not need to be spoken out loud or written down, unless you want it to be. A prayer can be said in your head using your own words.
- Saying 'Amen' at the end of a group prayer means saying to God that you agree with the prayer too.
- Take time to think about what you want to say to God before you pray. It might be easier to pray only one kind of a prayer at a time, such as a 'sorry' prayer or a 'thank you' prayer.
- Find a space where you are comfortable to say your prayer. You don't have to be on your own unless you want to be. The space could be on the stairs, at the end of the sofa, in the garden, at the table where you eat or anywhere you choose.
- Make time for your prayer if you can—it is better not to be rushed.
- Prayer can take place at any time and anywhere, but it helps if you are able to find a special space and a bit of time. If you can't find the space and time, you can talk to God when you are doing the things you usually do, such as walking to school, lying in bed or tidying your bedroom.

These guidelines can be reproduced on cards for each member of the group to take home. The print could be made very small so that the finished cards can be pocket-sized. Children enjoy seeing everyday objects in extreme sizes, such as miniature books or giant pencils, so making a 'guidelines' card in a miniature size would appeal.

The Lord's Prayer

Age guide: Over 10
Aim: To have a better understanding of the Lord's Prayer

Make available the two commonly used versions of the Lord's Prayer (printed below).

Traditional form

Our Father, who art in heaven,
Hallowed be thy name;
Thy kingdom come; thy will be done
On earth as it is in heaven.
Give us this day our daily bread.
And forgive us our trespasses,
As we forgive those who trespass against us.
And lead us not into temptation; but deliver us from evil.
For thine is the kingdom, the power, and the glory,
For ever and ever. Amen

Contemporary form

Our Father in heaven,
hallowed be your name.
Your kingdom come, your will be done
on earth as it is in heaven.
Give us today our daily bread.
Forgive us our sins as we forgive those who sin against us.
Save us from the time of trial and deliver us from evil.
For the kingdom, the power and the glory are yours
now and for ever. Amen

In small groups, each with a leader, work through the prayer, line by line, talking about what the words mean. Move on only when there is a collective understanding.

Discuss the version of the prayer that is regularly used in your church, which may be different from the two printed above. Which of the two versions above is most helpful to members of the group?

Write a new version of the prayer. This can be done in smaller groups. Keep the meaning of each sentence the same but use language that is more comfortable for the group to use.

Use the group's version the next time the Lord's Prayer is to be prayed.

Sharing a meal together

Share a meal of different types of bread. Have some simple spreads available to put on the bread.

Talk about how prayer is used to bless and thank God for our food. This kind of prayer is called a grace.

Ideas for reflection, prayer and sung worship

Reflection

Prayer is a conversation between God and ourselves; it is a direct link with God and should be respected. We should take time when we pray and allow time for God to speak to us. Taking time to be with God in prayer is special, and sharing prayers with others is a way we can worship as a community of God's people.

Take a moment now to think about how you pray. Think about the words you use and the way you address God. Think about how to listen to God and think about the many ways God uses to speak to you.

Prayer suggestions

Create a PowerPoint presentation based on the Lord's Prayer. Have different sentences of the prayer drifting on to the screen and lingering long enough to be read before drifting off again. The background should be made up of pastel colours or photographs that fit with the words. The presentation should run so that the Lord's Prayer appears on the screen three times. The first and third times should have the prayer in the usual order and the second in a random order. Try to set the presentation to music, working carefully on the timing as you do so.

Use your multimedia version of the Lord's Prayer to help people focus on the words and what they mean.

Hymns and songs

- There's a spirit in the air (CH; HAM; HP; RS)
- O Lord, hear my prayer (MP; RS; TS)
- Father, we love you (JP; MP; TS)
- Spirit of the living God (CH; JP; MP; HP; RS; TS)
- Meekness and majesty (CH; MP; TS)
- Make me a channel of your peace (CH; JP; MP; HP; RS; TS)

Taking it further

Church prayer request book

Create a prayer request book for your church. This is a book in which people can ask for prayers to be said for friends, family, neighbours or situations known to them. The requests can be left anonymously if desired. The book could be placed in a prominent position in the worship space so that groups can use it whenever they wish.

Association prayers

In order to help with personal prayer, create a tool that will organise your time so that all areas of life can be prayed for over a given period. Below is an example of how this might work. The idea is that it will eventually become natural to associate Friday with family and friends, so our personal prayers on Friday would bring to God any concerns or thanks that are related to family and friends.

- **Sunday** = S: Saviour (praising God)
- **Monday** = M: Me (prayers for ourselves)
- **Tuesday** = T: Thank you (giving thanks to God)
- **Wednesday** = W: World (prayers of intercession)
- **Thursday** = T: Those around us (people we know at school, at work and in our communities)
- **Friday** = F: Family and friends (people who are closest to us)
- **Saturday** = S: Sorry (saying sorry to God for the things we have done wrong)

Individuals can work out their own way of doing this. Other methods could be used, such as making up an acronym, creating a rhyme or using hands and fingers to guide the prayers.

— Theme 7 —

The wheels on the bus...

Suggested month
July

Season of the year
Summer

Christian season
Ordinary time

Colour
Green

Theme introduction

Along with August, July is a time when many of us think of holidays. Schools close for the summer, clubs take a break and there is a general feeling around that people are looking forward to the prospect of finding some space to be with their families and friends.

I grew up in a seaside town. Summer was a very busy time and many of those who lived in the town needed the seasonal employment in order to survive the following winter. The midweek church group that my sister and I attended took a break during the school holidays and we missed it greatly. However, there were always other things going on and my favourite event of summer was when the whole church went on a day trip together.

These trips were great adventures for the children and probably for adults, too. We always got the feeling that we had travelled far away when, in reality, we had not travelled far at all. The day usually included a big picnic, games, in which everyone seemed to take part, and somewhere of interest to visit. People seemed different: they were very smiley and they had time to talk to each other. Even those we did not know too well were all just part of the day. Worship either took place in the open air or in a borrowed church, depending on the weather. Visitors from other churches came to the worship and the singing was tremendous. I remember arriving home in the evening with the warm glow of tiredness and contentment all around me, too tired to do anything but sleep with a smile on my face.

This theme is about reclaiming the adventure of a day out together as a church family. Ideas include practical guidelines on early preparation for a day out, planning the theme and how to include members of the church family who often stay on the fringe of church life. Worship away from the church building is a highlight of the theme and can be as creative as your church wishes it to be, with the emphasis on accessibility for all.

Biblical context

When Jesus got out of the boat, he saw the large crowd. He felt sorry for them and healed everyone who was sick. That evening the disciples came to Jesus and said, 'This place is like a desert, and it is already late. Let the crowds leave, so they can go to the villages and buy some food.' Jesus replied, 'They don't have to leave. Why don't you give them something to eat?' But they said, 'We have only five small loaves of bread and two fish.' Jesus asked his disciples to bring the food to him, and he told the crowd to sit down on the grass. Jesus took the five loaves and the two fish. He looked up towards heaven and blessed the food. Then he broke the bread and handed it to his disciples, and they gave it to the people. After everyone had eaten all they wanted, Jesus' disciples

picked up twelve large baskets of leftovers. There were about five thousand men who ate, not counting the women and children.
MATTHEW 14:14–21

Reflection

There are many aspects to the story of the feeding of the five thousand—the large crowd that followed Jesus, Jesus' confidence that they could all be fed, the sharing of a picnic with an immense crowd and, in particular, the time that the crowd gave up to be with Jesus.

Immediately before this scene, Jesus had received the news of the death of his cousin, John. Already weary from teaching, this news must have upset him greatly. However, when the large crowd gathered to see him, he felt sorry for them, spent time with them and, as night fell, asked his disciples to share out the little bit of food they had managed to find. Jesus blessed the food and everyone in the crowd ate.

It is hard to imagine what the atmosphere would have been like on that day as Jesus talked with individuals. Perhaps groups chatted and shared their own stories with each other. Children probably played games and some may have been singing songs, while others would have enjoyed the space to sit and think and be at peace. We do not know what they did, but what we do know is that they spent time together; they ate together and they gave of their own time to be in Jesus' company.

Theme exploration

This theme is very different from the others and involves preparing for a big day out. The theme layout is therefore different, although the aim is the same—to worship God in a creative way.

To set the scene, a display will be needed to inspire people during the planning stage and as the plans move forward, but it also needs to be transportable to another place so that it can be present on the planned day out.

Have the display area draped with a patterned cloth. Add something that relates to the world around us, such as a handful of grass either from the garden or from the hedgerow. Add objects that make us think of summer, such as a bucket and spade, maps for travelling or a sun hat.

'Big day out' planning group

Set up a small planning group to plan the day out. It is not the sole responsibility of this group to organise the day; their job is to keep an overview of what needs to happen and to coordinate the involvement of others.

Agree the date, having checked that it does not clash with other events that might involve the church family. Publicise the date early and follow it up with booking forms, which should include details of any costs. All monies should be collected when places are booked.

Agree on a theme for the day. This could be related to any number of things, such as the destination (for example, the seaside), something of special interest in the area or about the season in which the day out will take place. The theme could be connected with your church, a special anniversary, a global event such as the Olympics, or a special event in your local area. Alternatively, a biblical theme could be used. A suitable Bible story might be the creation story: this would be of particular relevance if the day out is to an area of natural beauty. A good theme is one that is well known and easy to engage with, which has different aspects and angles that can be developed in a variety of ways.

Decide what shape the event will take. Will it be a visit to a nearby area with games organised and free time in the local town for small groups and families, with everyone gathering together for worship? Alternatively, will it be all about discovering something new together, with a hired venue and age-group-related activities exploring a theme? (A theme from this book could be used in this way.) Or, again, perhaps it might be a day purely for the church family to be together, with mixed-age group activities such as a treasure hunt, tournament-style games, giant picnic and worship together in the open.

If you are torn between various ideas, sound other people out and see how they feel. Having the right balance is important but not crucial: what is important is that everyone is included and people of all ages have been considered.

When the shape of the day is decided, make all the necessary bookings and arrangements in connection with transport, venues, tickets and obtaining visitor maps if they are needed. Approach individuals or groups within your church to work on various aspects of the day out, such as the food, games, treasure hunt, worship and so on. More is discussed below in connection with some of these items.

If the chosen destination is unfamiliar to the majority of the planning group, visit it to see where things are and how the area is set up. If, on the day of the trip, options are to be offered that involve walking to different places, walk the routes, make a note of the timings and check access on the routes for people who are less mobile. Find out what is on offer in the area if people are to have free time to visit the locality. Make a connection with any church contacts in the area: they will be invaluable in helping with local knowledge, and perhaps one day the favour can be returned.

Find out at an early stage the contact details and locations of places that might be needed in an emergency, such as hospital, police station, dentist, chemist and supermarket. One member of the planning group should keep all of this information together in one place so that it is readily available if it is needed later. Gathering this information at an early stage will prevent a sudden panic nearer to the event, if it should get forgotten in the busyness of the final preparations.

Ask the person in your church who is responsible for insurance to contact the insurance company and tell them of the planned day out. They will advise on your current cover and whether any additional cover is needed.

If guests from outside the immediate church family are to be invited, this should be done well in advance.

Practical advice

- Everyone should be given a small card showing the mobile phone numbers of one or two of the organisers who are also attending the day.
- Consent forms for those under the age of 18 will be needed if they are unaccompanied by a parent or guardian.
- If the day involves being dispersed, agree a meeting point for people who get lost and a time for everyone to gather together.
- If you are going to an attraction, check that there are seating facilities for people who get tired.
- Make sure the venue will allow you to eat your own food there.

Catering

Arrange for a small group, perhaps two or three people, to take responsibility for coordinating the catering. Encourage them to involve as many others as is practically possible, especially if food is to be prepared in advance. It might be possible to link the food in with the theme of the day. (See below for suggestions on sharing a meal together.) Make sure that any food hygiene guidelines the church has in place are followed.

Games and roaming activities

A second small group (again, up to three people) could be asked to organise the games and out-and-about activities if these are planned. Some groups within the church or connected to the church may have a natural leaning towards this kind of activity and will have the necessary expertise and equipment. If such activities are planned, it is always good to have alternatives prepared for those who are unable or unwilling to play the games. Some people will simply enjoy watching and will participate by cheering and encouraging when necessary. Not everyone feels the need to be busy all the time.

Sharing a meal together

There are several options to pursue for sharing a meal. More than one meal may need to be considered, depending on the distance to travel and whether it is a half-day or whole-day event. Here are some suggestions to get the thinking started.

- People could bring their own picnics.
- People could find food at the venue, although some might not be able to afford to eat out, and it does depend on what the destination has to offer.
- A gathered picnic could be offered, with different people being responsible for bringing different elements of the picnic to be shared.
- A group could meet the evening before the day out and prepare a picnic. Some forward planning would need to be in place to spread the work around.
- A church local to the destination could be asked to supply a meal. A local church would also be a good back-up for bad weather, whatever the chosen food option.

Ideas for reflection, prayer and sung worship

Reflection

Ask someone to take pictures of the day, using a digital camera. The pictures should be of places and things rather than people. The pictures will be memories of the day and can be shown using a projector as part of the reflection on the day. The pictures can be shown on the day if the group are meeting in a church to worship or at some later date.

Reflection quiz sheet

Create a quiz for families or groups to do throughout the day. The quiz could include questions that refer to items of interest in the area or could be a collection of pictures of items to be 'found' in the area. The pictures could be hand-drawn sketches or photographic images taken on a previous visit.

Gift box

Give younger members of the group a gift box or gift bag (available from card shops or supermarkets) and ask them to collect things that they found special on the day. Items could include a leaf, some sand, sweet wrapper, a leaflet, a piece of sheep's wool, some grass, a stone or shell and so on. The collecting will need to be supervised to ensure that health and safety are maintained.

When everyone is together, read Matthew 14:13–21 and ask if there were any moments in the day that resonated with the passage.

Prayer suggestions

Prayers could focus on the theme chosen for the day. They can be drawn from the experiences of the day or can be prepared in advance. Any prayers for the church family should include those present as well as those who were not able to be part of the day out.

Colours prayer walk

The idea of this walk is to notice things by their colour and to thank God for them throughout the course of the day. Choose from a range of colours, such as blue, green, orange, grey, red, yellow, black, pink and brown. Ask everyone to choose five colours from the range on offer.

To help people remember the colours they are looking for, provide a colour aid, such as stickers, wool lengths, ribbon pieces, colours drawn on to a card and so on. Whichever method you use, make sure you have enough pieces cut in each colour for people to choose.

As they walk through their day, ask people to focus on their particular colours, to stop when they see something in one of those colours and give thanks to God for whatever it is.

Alternatively, prepare a prayer walk based on the area and the theme for the day.

A prayer before the day

Dear God,
As we listen to your words,
As we plan for a special time together,
As we think of each other,
As we think of you,
Help us to remember that you are close, guiding us in all we do.
We offer our preparation for this day, in Jesus' name.
Amen

Prayer on the day

If everyone is travelling together by coach, meet at the church and share a prayer, offering the day to God. If people are making their own way to the destination, arrange a meeting place and time so that a prayer can be shared when everyone is gathered. It is important that this day of togetherness is both God-centred and blessed by God.

Hymns and songs

- Lord of all hopefulness (CH; JP; MP; HAM; HP; RS)
- Our God is a great big God (JP)
- For the beauty of the earth (CH; JP; MP; HAM; HP; RS)
- Moses, I know you're the man (HP; RS)
- All over the world (JP; MP; TS)
- One more step (CH; JP; HP; RS)
- For I'm building a people of power (JP; MP; TS)

Plan ahead

Set up a worship planning group for the event. This may or may not involve the regular worship leader(s) (they might enjoy being participants of a different kind on this occasion). Link the theme for sung worship to the theme for the day out.

Plan the outline of sung worship, deciding what will be included and how it can be included. For example, it is not easy to have instrumental music accompanying hymns when worshipping on the beach. However, voices are transportable, so singing can be included.

Involve others in specific areas of the worship. Perhaps the church has a choir or singing group that could be asked to lead the singing. Alternatively, an amateur dramatics group could organise a brief drama, or a youth group could be invited to organise a creative talk. The more people who are involved, the better. The work is shared and there will be more enjoyment for everyone.

If other churches, or members of your own church not coming for the whole day out, are to be invited to the worship, make sure they know the date well in advance.

Plan for the worship to be lively, upbeat and not too long. All age groups will be present for the whole time and this should be remembered in the planning.

Taking it further

- Approach neighbouring churches with which there is an established connection and invite them to join the day out. Set up a joint group from both churches to plan the event.
- Write up your experience and share it with churches in the neighbourhood or others a little distance away; offer to host another church's day out.
- Arrange a gathering after worship or an evening get-together at a future date to share the experiences of the day. Encourage people to bring their photographs or memories of the day to share (perhaps someone will have made a video of the day). Those who were not able to take part in the trip may particularly appreciate a gathering of this kind.

*

— Theme 8 —

Quiet places

Suggested month
August

Season of the year
Summer

Christian season
Ordinary time

Colour
Green

Theme introduction

Cornflowers and poppies grow side by side with grain crops in the fields in August. Grains are harvested and vegetables and flowers in the gardens are straining to stay fresh in the parched earth, their colours still vibrant. Blackberries are in the hedgerows, crabs and shrimps are sought in rockpools and the tantalising smell of barbeques fills the evening air as we enjoy the long days of high summer. The air is still and a hazy quietness pervades, even in the places where people are gathered and having fun.

Many people go away on holiday. Some are seeking fun and excitement and others are seeking quiet places, places to be alone with family and friends, places to be simply at one with nature. Some people do not have a holiday away, but finding quiet places is something that has become important to many of us.

Churches can be very busy places, even in the summer months, when many members of the church family are away. Finding a quiet place in church is often hard, and this theme looks at creating quiet places that can be encountered by those who regularly attend your church, as well as summer visitors.

In her book *Creative Ideas for Quiet Corners* (Barnabas, 2008), Lynn Chambers describes a quiet corner for children or adults as 'a rare place where they can simply be' (p. 9). Lynn uses multisensory prayer to create quiet places, and this theme encapsulates the essence of Lynn's book in creating quiet places in a church and encouraging everyone to take time to be with God.

Biblical context

Straight away, Jesus made his disciples get into a boat and start back across the lake. But he stayed until he had sent the crowds away. Then he went up on a mountain where he could be alone and pray. Later that evening, he was still there.

MATTHEW 14:22–23

Very early the next morning, Jesus got up and went to a place where he could be alone and pray. Simon and the others started looking for him. And when they found him, they said, 'Everyone is looking for you!'

MARK 1:35–37

But so many people were coming and going that Jesus and the apostles did not even have a chance to eat. Then Jesus said, 'Let's go to a place where we can be alone and get some rest.' They left in a boat for a place where they could be alone.

MARK 6:31–32

Reflection

It is clear to see, from the three passages above, that Jesus found value in being alone with God. He used the quiet places he found to talk to God and to listen to God. In the reading from Matthew, Jesus sends the crowds and his disciples away because he wants to be alone with God. Time passes; when the disciples come back to look for Jesus, they find that he is still where they left him.

When Jesus tells the crowd how to pray, he tells them to 'go into a room alone' and 'pray to your Father in private' (Matthew 6:6). Being alone with God need not mean being still and away from others; it simply means allowing our thoughts to be in communion with God.

Sometimes, quiet places are needed to allow us an opportunity to gather ourselves, to give ourselves time to let our thoughts settle. They provide some valuable space, helping us to find the inner calm that enables us to cope with the many pressures of everyday life.

Being alone with God, creating a quiet time and allowing ourselves to be quiet, is a gift we can give to ourselves, and we can do it in community with others. We can be still or active, but our minds are with God and our hands can help our heads as we pray.

Theme exploration

To set the scene, have a display area draped with a cloth of any colour. Add something that relates to the world around us, such as some blackberries, grains or tomatoes from the garden. Have some books to read or objects to represent other relaxing activities that people like to do in quiet times. Place a bowl of water on the table and some pebbles nearby.

Plan ahead

It is hoped that all ages will be able to participate in the worship, and age-specific suggestions are given below. However, if you feel that some groups would benefit more from being in their own space, the suggestions below will still be valuable.

Different areas of the church will be set up as quiet places. Multisensory prayer activities will be available in each of these areas, along with an explanation of how to use them. The quiet places will need to be planned and set up in advance, and it would be helpful if a small worship group was brought together to do this. Given below are some suggestions for prayer in the quiet places, but you may wish to add suggestions from the group.

The quiet places worship can take place in any part of your church premises. Prepare a number of different places in which the prayer activities will be based. Depending on the size of the congregation, it is likely that a number of people will visit each space at the same time.

Some rooms are small and can only hold one activity. Bigger spaces, such as the church or hall, can host several quiet places. Think about using spaces usually reserved for other purposes, such as the vestibule, the coffee lounge or the book corner. It is good if all the chosen spaces connect with each other in some way, so arrange for doors to be kept open to enable people to move quietly and easily from one place to another.

If there are church gardens and the weather is fine, think about setting up some or all of the quiet places around the gardens.

Taking all these factors into consideration, decide how many quiet places there are to be and what themes will be used.

Themes could be based on Bible passages such as the 'I am' sayings of Jesus (for example, John 15:1, 'I am the true vine', or John 10:14, 'I am the good shepherd'). They could be based on general themes such as creation, water, journeys and so on; or they could be based on intercessional prayer subjects, such as different areas of the world, considering both the joys and the difficulties in those areas.

Setting the scene

When the places have been chosen, use draped cloths, lamps or pictures associated with the prayer activity to change the image of the space, so that they will all look and feel different. Arrange to have seating available in each space: some chairs and an occasional rug will add to the ambiance of the space. The seating can be spaced out according to the room available in each quiet area.

Each quiet place should contain a mixture of the following:

- A table covered with a coloured cloth. Other items can be placed upon it.
- Pictures from magazines, books or your own sources.
- Poems for people to read and use in their personal prayers.
- Objects of any shape and size, as long as they are suitable for people to handle. Choose tactile objects that will resonate with the senses, such as smooth pebbles, sand or freshly cut grass.
- Candles in suitable candle holders to minimise risk.
- Bible passage references, which could be copied out several times.
- Craft materials.
- Bibles and books.
- Music, if appropriate.

Some food and drink items could be used, but be mindful of food allergies and food colourings, which can cause problems for some people. (See below for health and safety advice.)

There are many ways to explore themes. The idea of the quiet spaces is to provide a number of items that will resonate differently with people, inspiring them and taking them on their own spiritual journey to a quiet place with God. Once you have decided on your themes, the creativity can begin. If more help is needed, see *Creative Ideas for Quiet Corners* by Lynn Chambers.

Theme example: 'I am the true vine'

- Drape a purple or green cloth over a table for the base.
- Suspend a central piece of rope or twine from the ceiling (or place a substantial twig in a pot). A number of vine leaves pre-cut from card could be made available. Each visitor to the space could write his or her name on a leaf and attach it, using sticky tack or a paperclip, to the central 'vine' as a visible representation that they are part of the church.
- Print out the words from John 15:1 and display them on the table or on a wall beside the table.
- Place pictures of a vine on the cloth.
- Scatter raisins on the cloth, or place a bunch of seedless grapes on a plate, along with a card inviting people to eat a raisin or grape. Ask people to taste the sweetness of the fruit and think about other fruit that grows from the soil.
- Write a prayer to leave by the picture of the vine for people to use in the quiet place, and provide copies of the prayer for people to take away with them.
- Make available some plain paper and some colouring pens or pencils, to allow people to draw their own pictures.
- Display an old rope with loosened strands, symbolising a twisted vine, and a card with some instructions inviting people to think about the vine and consider the way it grows like a twisted rope.

The quiet spaces worship

The week before the quiet places worship is to take place, tell everyone how the worship will happen, so that they are prepared on the day. Hand out information sheets as people arrive, including an introduction to the worship and an explanation about quiet spaces and how they work, where in the building each one is set up, what to expect and what not to expect. It might be helpful if some members of the worship group are available to answer questions before the worship begins.

- Have some quiet music playing as people arrive and gather for worship.
- Sing a gentle hymn or song together. A song that helps people to collect their thoughts and moves them from their busy lives to the quiet peacefulness of the day's worship would be highly suitable.
- Say a prayer to gather people together into the space at the centre of the worship area. Light a candle or several candles and pause for a moment before sending everyone to the quiet places to continue their worship.

If information sheets have been produced, there will be no need to explain about the quiet places: you can simply let people go and find them. If the quiet places are tucked away and therefore potentially difficult to find, have a few well-placed maps or signs on the walls to help people find their way around.

Health and safety

Care must be taken to ensure that those using the quiet places remain safe. Ensure that all equipment used is safe and suitable for the age and abilities of those using it. Special care needs to be taken when using small objects that could be swallowed, hard objects that could be thrown and candles, which could become a fire hazard. Ensure that any quiet places using these objects are supervised.

Age-specific theme activities

Finding the colours

Age guide: Under 5
Aim: To be still and quiet

Ask the children to lie on the floor and listen to gentle music. How does the music make them feel? Ask them to listen for a while longer. What colour does it remind them of? When the music finishes, ask the children to listen to the sounds in the room. Perhaps they would like to close their eyes while they do this.

Have ready a basket full of colourful shapes made from materials that can float, such as small pieces of different coloured ribbons or coloured card cut into fish shapes. Anything can be used, as long as it will float. Invite the children to quietly choose an item from the basket that most looks like the colour of the music for them.

Place a large bowl of water on the floor. Say a prayer together and ask the children to float their colours on the water. When the prayer is over, move the bowl to another place. The children can choose another colour from the basket to take home with them if they wish.

A quiet space

Age guide: Under 10
Aim: To create a quiet place

Either set up a tent in which the group can sit or make a parachute tent. To make a parachute tent, ask everyone to hold on to the edges of a parachute (with their knuckles on top and their thumbs tucked under the chute for safety). Start to move the chute up and down rhythmically. On a given signal, such as the count of three, everyone hoists the parachute into the air and, as it comes down, takes a step forward, bringing the parachute down behind them while facing into the centre of the circle. As the parachute continues to descend, everyone sits down on the edge of parachute that they have been holding. Everyone should now be inside the parachute tent.

Ask everyone to be quiet. What can they hear around them? What noises can be heard in the room? Share a prayer. Keep the group inside the quiet place for as long as they find helpful.

Sharing a meal together

Set out the refreshment area as a quiet space. Think about the use of food in the Bible—how it was part of festivals as well as everyday life. Place cards showing food-related Bible passages around the food. Make jugs of drink available for people to help themselves. Play quiet music in the background.

Ideas for reflection, prayer and sung worship

Reflection

Have gentle music playing as people gather together in the main worship space. Ask people to sit in a space on their own. Continue to play the music.

Read Matthew 14:22–23. Remind people that Jesus spent time on his own to pray. Ask everyone to think about the space immediately around them, reminding them that it is not empty and that God is close. Ask them to think of a place inside themselves that is warm.

Ask everyone to sit together, as close as they can. No one should be sitting on their own.

Read Mark 6:31–33. Remind people that Jesus and the disciples went to a place where they could be alone together. Ask everyone to think of those who are close to them now. Can they feel the warmth of the person next to them? Ask everyone to think about how close God is to them right now.

Prayer suggestions

Draw the worship to a close by adding an item from each of the quiet places to the display area. Have a number of tealight candles lit around the room or church. Use the following short liturgy.

Leader: At times Jesus chose to pray alone and at times he chose to pray with others. Today we have been scattered, like the candles in this space, throughout the church in quiet places. We have been alone with God and with our thoughts.

Ask the people nearest to the candles to bring them slowly to the display area, still lit.

Leader: Now we come together, like these candles, as a community of God's people.
    Let us be for ever in the presence of your light Lord, and be with us now as we carry the thoughts of today with us into the week ahead. Amen

Hymns and songs

- A new commandment I give unto you (JP; MP; RS; TS)
- As the deer pants for the water (CH; MP; TS)
- Be still, for the presence of the Lord (CH; JP; MP; RS; TS)
- Spirit of the living God (CH; JP; MP; HP; RS; TS)
- Ubi caritas et amor (CH; RS)
- Laudate omnes gentes (RS)

Taking it further

Open your church to the wider community and invite people to experience the quiet places. Issue a press release or put an advert in a local paper, telling the local community about the quiet places and advertising when the church will be open for the quiet places to be used.

Fruit cocktail

Suggested month
September

Season of the year
Autumn

Christian season
Harvest

Colour
Green

Theme introduction

For many people, September feels like the end of summer, but at first the days can still be warm. Towards the end of the month, however, the days become damper and feel shorter and a sense of autumn is in the air. In the gardens, by the sides of the roads and in the woodlands, fruits are ripe and ready to eat, squirrels gather nuts and seeds for the long winter ahead and gardeners store their root vegetables in sand-filled boxes.

The first morning mists of autumn roll in at the end of the month and some people's thoughts turn to winter holidays in faraway places. Harvest festivals are celebrated in schools and churches and harvest suppers take place as the evenings begin to draw in.

This theme takes the season of harvest and builds on it as the focus is shifted from local harvests to the situation in other parts of the world. Fruit is used to introduce thinking about other countries—

looking at the produce they grow and harvest. The theme embarks on a tour, considering the different fruits, the countries from which they come and the people who live in those countries.

Connections may be made with different members of the church family and their own families and friends and, hopefully, lots of stories will be heard. This theme is designed to be fun and to create a way for everyone to learn, play and pray together as a church family.

Biblical context

So God created humans to be like himself; he made men and women. God gave them his blessing and said: Have a lot of children! Fill the earth with people and bring it under your control. Rule over the fish in the sea, the birds in the sky, and every animal on the earth. I have provided all kinds of fruit and grain for you to eat. And I have given the green plants as food for everything else that breathes. These will be food for animals, both wild and tame, and for birds.

GENESIS 1:27–30

As long as the earth remains, there will be planting and harvest, cold and heat; winter and summer, day and night.

GENESIS 8:22

Reflection

At the very beginning of the Bible, Genesis tells the story of creation. God created all living things—trees, plants and grains, fish and birds, animals and reptiles. He made all kinds of varieties of each, including some that still remain unknown to us. God created a complete cocktail of species, but every single one has a purpose: all things were made to be in harmony with each other and had a reason for being. We read that some species were created to be food and others to benefit from eating that food. Some plants provide shade to protect crops and some benefit from that shading. Some can survive unaided and others need tending, but all are important and special in God's eyes.

As the crown of his creation, God created human beings. However, in Genesis 6:1–7 we read that God became angry with the people he had created because of the way they behaved towards each other, and he decided to make a clean start. Apart from Noah, his family and two of each species of each animal, God allowed all living creatures to be drowned in the flood (Genesis 6:9—7:23). In Genesis 8:21–22, God speaks to Noah, who has just emerged from the ark that saved him and his family from the great flood. God promises Noah that the diversity and richness of all life that inhabits the earth will never again be threatened in this way. God infinitely values creation with its colour, variety and vitality.

Theme exploration

To set the scene, have a display area draped with a green cloth. Add something that relates to the world around us, such as fruits from gardens, some snails, a small wormery or pictures of misty days. Add pictures of fruits from around the world, or the fruits themselves.

Fruit is used throughout this theme. The fruit doesn't have to be fresh: the packaging of tinned fruit usually shows its place of origin and can therefore provide the necessary information.

Plan ahead

Decide in advance which fruits and which countries are to be the focus for the theme. Using a library or the internet, gather some general information about each country from which the fruits come (probably about four or five facts). Information could include details of the climate, the country's flag, facts about how people live, other foods that are part of the staple diet, the dominant religion, a description of games played by children, a brief history and so on—in fact, anything that would be of interest and help to form an impression that distinguishes the country from others.

Matching game

Aim: To identify the country of origin of fruits from around the world

Place several tables around the room for people to visit. Number the tables.

On each table, display a map of the world and a selection of different types of fruit (or pictures of fruit) from one particular country. Include a table with fruits that are native to the United Kingdom.

Divide into smaller mixed-age groups and give each group a pen and paper. The groups have to visit each table and write down the table's number, the names of the different types of fruit and which country they think the fruits are from.

Fruit cocktail

Aim: To discover more about the countries where some fruits are grown

Start by playing the matching game above. When the fruits and their countries have been matched, place the pre-prepared sheets with the country information on the relevant tables.

Allocate one group to each table, and ask them to read the information about the country represented by the fruits on their table. Invite them to talk among themselves about the similarities and differences between the country from which the fruits come and the country in which we ourselves live.

When the groups have had enough time to do this, come back together as a whole and invite each group to introduce their fruit and its country to everyone else.

Each group should choose one fact about their table's country, which they would like included in the 'countries' prayer (see pp. 112–113). The prayer line will be said by a member of the group and should include the name of the country and the prayer request. For example, 'We pray for Colombia, from where the uchuva (cape gooseberry) comes. The country is very beautiful, but war makes life difficult for those who live there. Please be with the people of Colombia as they live their day-to-day lives.'

Age-specific theme activities

All the senses

Age guide: Under 5
Aim: To explore different fruits using our five senses

Set out a selection of fresh fruits. Include some familiar fruits, such as apples or oranges, and some not-so-familiar ones, such as mangos and lychees.

Leave the fruits whole and allow the children to explore each one with all their senses. What does it feel like? Can they smell the fruit? Does it have or make a sound? Can they guess what it will look like inside?

Cut the fruit open and invite the children to taste it. This might be quite challenging for some children, so have cups of water ready to drink if the taste is not liked.

Fruit tasting

Age guide: Under 5
Aim: To try a different food and to see where it comes from

Have a number of fruits prepared for tasting. The fruits can be fresh, tinned or frozen (defrosted). Which ones do the children recognise and which tastes do they like?

Talk about where the different types of fruit come from. Ask the children if there is any fruit growing in their gardens or near where they live.

Fruit smelling

Age guide: Under 10
Aim: To recognise different types of fruit by their smell

Place a number of easily recognised fruits, cut open, in lidded boxes, but ensure that they cannot be seen. Number the boxes. The children should work in pairs, with one of the pair closing their eyes while the other holds the box beneath their nose for them to sniff. The children should try to identify the fruit by its smell. They can keep notes if this is helpful.

An alternative is to place a whole fruit inside a small fabric bag for the children to feel. Tell them that they will need to be very gentle with the fruits. Make as many fruit bags as required and ask each child to identify the fruit by its feel and shape. Pass the bags around gently for as long as the activity remains interesting.

If there is time, invite the children to try the fruit tasting activity above.

Fruit footprints

Age guide: Over 10
Aim: To see how far fruit travels

This activity uses the fruits from the 'Fruit cocktail' activity (pp. 108–109). Note the names of the countries from which these fruits came. Using a world map, calculate how far each fruit has travelled to get to our shops. Which fruit has travelled the furthest? Have any fruits that could have been grown in our own country travelled from another country? What is the total mileage travelled by the fruit cocktail?

Fair trade issues

Age guide: Over 10
Aim: To understand how fairly traded fruit can change lives

Fair trade is an ever-growing concern for many people. Fruit is one of the biggest fair trade product ranges available, and bananas, in particular, have made a huge impact. In 2006 a major supermarket chain announced that they would sell only fairly traded bananas. As that chain sells more than ten million bananas a week, that one act more than doubled the demand for fairly traded bananas.

Those who grow fruits for the fair trade market are usually part of fair trade cooperatives. The Fairtrade Foundation ensures that farmers are paid a decent price for their fruits and the cooperatives ensure that everyone receives a decent wage. The Foundation also works with the farmers and cooperatives by supporting reinvestment into farms and communities. In many cases, it enables the workers to become co-owners of the farms on which they work, giving them both stability and a future.

Discover more about how the fair trade movement has changed the lives of those who work for the farms that supply the fruit and other products for the fair trade industry.

Sharing a meal together

Make fruit kebabs using a mixture of familiar and less-familiar fruit.

Set up a smoothies and fruit juice bar after worship. Have a variety of drinks available using fair trade fruits and fruit juices. Recipes can be found in books or on the internet.

Make fruit salad and serve it in small bowls, using a mixture of familiar and less-familiar fruit.

Ideas for reflection, prayer and sung worship

Reflection

Use a meditation based on harvest or the fruits of the earth. A hymn or several verses of a hymn read out slowly would make a suitable meditation. Play some music quietly to help people focus.

Anthologies of poems and meditations are readily available from book suppliers.

Prayer suggestions

Countries prayer

This prayer is a focus on the countries that the groups have been thinking about. Ask each group to choose one fact that they have discovered about the country, which they would like everyone to pray for.

When everyone is assembled to pray, place a large basket in a central position. Place a label with the words 'Fruit Cocktail' on or near the basket.

The prayer leader begins the prayer with intercessions for general concerns. At a suitable point in the prayer, the leader places a small globe or symbol of the world next to the basket. This is a signal for each group in turn to share the prayer lines they have written for the countries they have been thinking about. When the prayer line has been said, a member of the group places the fruit and the country's name in the basket. All groups should take a turn and all countries should be included in the prayer, including the country in which we live.

After the prayer lines for each country have been spoken, the leader gathers the prayers together by emphasising the point that although all of the fruits are different, they are all fruit and part of the one worldwide fruit cocktail. In the same way, all of the countries are different but part of one world. The leader closes by offering the prayers to God.

Use the themes of fruit and harvest to help focus your prayers.

Hymns and songs

Choose hymns, songs and choruses that are related to harvest or to the people of the world, such as the examples below.

- Let all the world in every corner sing (CH; MP; HAM; HP; RS)
- Let all God's people join in one (RS)
- O Lord my God, when I in awesome wonder (CH; JP; MP; RS; TS)
- O give thanks to the Lord (JP; MP)
- Think of a world without any flowers (CH; JP; HP; RS)
- The love of God is broad like beach and meadow (RS)

Taking it further

Become a fair trade church. The Fairtrade Foundation can give advice on how to become a fair trade church. Contact the Foundation at www.fairtrade.org.uk for further advice, or contact the relevant department in your denominational church headquarters.

＊

— Theme 10 —

Surviving the storm

Suggested month
October

Season of the year
Autumn

Christian season
Ordinary time

Colour
Green

Theme introduction

October feels like autumn. The leaves on the trees are fantastic shades of red, orange and rusty brown. Chestnuts fall from their husks and conker competitions are all but over. Fields are bare after being ploughed and left to lie fallow over the winter, and bees and wasps are long forgotten. The outside eating areas of restaurants, bars and coffee shops have all been stowed away and seaside kiosks are boarded up, ready for the winter storms.

Sudden storms bring thunder and lightning as weather fronts compete for dominance in the atmosphere. People turn their faces against the wind and schoolchildren pull their coats tight around them; there is a real sense that the elements are closing in and we will soon be under siege from the weather around us.

This theme explores how we can feel battered by the storms of life in today's society. Young people and children often feel windswept and knocked sideways by the contradictory messages that they continually receive. Pressure is put on them to grow up too fast, to be model children and to do what is right in everyone's eyes. Peer groups pressurise young people in so many ways and society itself, often taking its lead from the media, heaps its expectations and negativity upon them daily. Children and young people are faced with exams at early ages and are pressured by the education system to make choices that will affect the rest of their lives. Some are pressurised by parents, too.

As adults, we too are constantly battered by these storms, facing similar contradictory messages from peer groups, the media and our own families. We are expected to be good parents, husbands, wives, sons, daughters and employees. We should spend more time with our children, but we must work longer to provide all the electronic gadgets that are needed (so the adverts tell us) to survive modern life. We should be with our loved ones in our leisure time but must also be sociable members of the team in which we work. We should cook like celebrity chefs and grow our own vegetables, but also eat out regularly. We should go to the theatre, relax on the beach, be well read, watch all the latest reality TV programmes, participate in extreme sports and attend the school sports day. The list is endless!

This theme acknowledges the pressures that life's storms bring, whatever their size. It reminds everyone that they do not have to face the storms alone. God helps us both directly and through others, and we need to remember to hand ourselves over to God at such times so that he might carry us through the storms.

Begin by welcoming each other. The worship theme brings everyone together to a place where the storm is stilled for a time and God can speak and be heard in the quieter places of life.

Biblical context

One day, Jesus and his disciples got into a boat, and he said, 'Let's cross the lake.' They started out, and while they were sailing across, he went to sleep. Suddenly a storm struck the lake, and the boat started sinking. They were in danger. So they went to Jesus and woke him up, 'Master, Master! We are about to drown!' Jesus got up and ordered the wind and waves to stop. They obeyed, and everything was calm. Then Jesus asked the disciples, 'Don't you have any faith?' But they were frightened and amazed. They said to each other, 'Who is this? He can give orders to the wind and the waves, and they obey him!'

LUKE 8:22–25

Jesus said to his disciples: I tell you not to worry about your life! Don't worry about having something to eat or wear. Life is more than food or clothing. Look at the crows! They don't plant or harvest, and they don't have storehouses or barns. But God takes care of them. You are much more important than any birds. Can worry make you live longer? If you don't have power over small things, why worry about everything else? Look how the wild flowers grow! They don't work hard to make their clothes. But I tell you that Solomon with all his wealth wasn't as well clothed as one of these flowers. God gives such beauty to everything that grows in the fields, even though it is here today and thrown into a fire tomorrow. Won't he do even more for you? You have such little faith! Don't keep worrying about having something to eat or drink. Only people who don't know God are always worrying about such things. Your Father knows what you need. But put God's work first, and these things will be yours as well.

LUKE 12:22–31

Reflection

The Bible passages above are very different from each other. The first is about Jesus responding to a request from his disciples and the second shows Jesus teaching them about God's love.

When Jesus and the disciples decided to take a boat to the other side of Lake Galilee, the water was calm and Jesus rested as the boat sailed across the water. However, while Jesus slept, a storm blew up. This happened so suddenly that it took the disciples by surprise and they were frightened. There seems to be an element of panic in the story, which is surprising, as some of the disciples were fishermen and must have sailed through many storms. Unsure about what to do, they wake Jesus and tell him that they are about to drown.

Jesus, woken suddenly from his sleep, perhaps seems a little irritated as he tells the wind and the waves to calm down and then asks the disciples, 'Don't you have any faith?' The disciples are surprised by the power that Jesus displays.

The second passage describes Jesus teaching his disciples about how God will take care of them. Jesus tells them not to worry about the things they need. He reminds them that God takes care of all the flowers and the birds. He tells them to stop thinking so much about themselves and to concentrate on working for God.

Jesus knows that life is hard and, at times, the smaller issues do cloud the bigger picture. Jesus is not telling the disciples that God will give them everything they want, but rather that God knows their needs and will provide. This message is as relevant for us today as it was for Jesus' first disciples.

Theme exploration

To set the scene, have a display area draped with a cloth that depicts autumn. Add some items relating to autumn and to the world around us, such as fallen leaves of different colours, conkers and acorns. Add to the display pictures of rough seas and trees being blown by the wind.

Welcome to worship

Aim: To encourage people to meet each other at the start of worship with an ice breaker greeting game

Depending on the number of people gathered, either work as one group or in smaller mixed-age groups. Ask everyone to stand in a circle, facing each other. Everyone then places something personal and recognisable to them (such as a pair of gloves, a bag or a book) on the floor behind them. If people are anxious about placing their personal possessions out of sight in this way, have a number of pictures or postcards available for people to choose from. They can then place the picture they have chosen on the floor as their marker. Select one person as the starter for each group.

The starter takes a step forward and turns to face the person next to them on their left. They greet that person by saying their name and the words 'Welcome to worship today.' For example, Jean would say to David, 'David, welcome to worship today.' The starter then moves clockwise around the circle to face the third person in the circle and greets them in the same way. As the starter moves clockwise again to greet the fourth person, the person who was originally second in the circle follows the starter and greets the person immediately on their left. This procession of greeting continues until everyone has greeted everyone else, and everyone has been greeted by everyone else.

When the starter gets back to their marker, they remain by it until they have been greeted by everyone else in the circle. Then they pick up their marker and take it to the display area as a symbol that they have been welcomed to worship today. Everyone else follows in turn with their own markers, and the final two people go together.

NB: The greeting could take place in a line rather than a circle, if preferred.

Age-specific theme activities

Something new

Age guide: Under 5
Aim: To learn to do something new with help from someone else

Present a number of activities for the group to try. Choose things that they are unlikely to have tried before, which could include games brought from home or challenges such as those listed below. The expectation is that the tasks will be easier to do if they help each other. For example, standing on one foot for a whole minute is difficult when you are very young, but, if you are able to hold on to someone else's hand, it becomes easier.

- Stand on one foot for one minute.
- Take ten steps forward with your eyes closed.
- Play a game of Tiddlywinks or Jumping Frogs (or any game that needs two people).
- Thread five large beads on to a shoelace.
- Sit on the floor and get up without putting your hands on the floor.
- Complete a jigsaw puzzle (choose an appropriate size for children's abilities).

When a challenge has been completed, everyone should applaud. This will show that it is good to let others help us and that, together, we can achieve things.

Jesus calms the storm (theatre-style)

Age guide: Under 10
Aim: To understand the story of Jesus calming the storm by working together

This activity involves working as a group to create a model theatre and the characters in the story. The children can then use the theatre to tell the story—similar to a shadow theatre but with colour! The model will be on a table top and the children can act out the story by moving characters in from the sides of the model.

Plan ahead

Beforehand, find a large box to make the main theatre. Cut away one side of the box, leaving a big opening through which the story will be viewed. If time is likely to be short, the basic scenery of sky, sea and horizon could be painted inside the box in advance.

Make the characters and boat and fix them to the ends of thin sticks, such as garden canes, so that the character is upright when the stick is held horizontally. The sticks need to be long enough for the character to be seen on stage, while the other end of the stick is being held in a child's hand outside the box. Clouds and waves can also be made in the same way. Cut openings at the sides of the box (the wings of the stage) for the sticks to pass through.

Tell the story

When the theatre, scenery, characters, boat, waves and clouds are ready, read through Luke 8:22–25 (see p. 116). Let the children practise telling the story with the theatre and characters. If you prefer, let the children act out the story using the theatre while the passage is read by one of the leaders.

As the children work together and discuss the story, talk to them about how God helps them when they have difficult times. Jesus' power to calm the storm came from God.

The table-top theatre can be kept to be used at other times. Additional characters, props and scenery can easily be added.

A stormy and sunny montage

Age guide: Over 10
Aim: To name concerns in general terms

Plan ahead

Cut out stories or headlines from newspapers throughout the week (a number of people could do this, to give lots of stories and a variety of viewpoints). Choose stories showing the 'storms of life'— concerns, worries or anything that could present a difficulty for someone. Be aware that it is not just the big stories that are part of the storms of life; smaller worries often have the most impact on our lives. Also, make a collection of 'sunny' stories that show kindness, general good feeling and good news both for people and the environment.

Having several different cuttings about a particular story will work well. Take care when choosing stories and be mindful of the age of participants, as well as any recent events in people's personal lives that could make them particularly vulnerable in this activity.

Provide a number of small pieces of paper, some white and some coloured, and pens with which to write.

Make the montage

Divide into small groups and give each group a selection of the 'stormy' newspaper stories. The cuttings should be placed in the centre of the table around which the group is based. Ask each group to talk about the stories and, using the white papers, to add any general concerns they have. These can be placed face down if they wish. Remember, this activity should not make people feel uncomfortable.

At a suitable point, give each group the 'sunny' stories and ask them to place the cuttings around the outside or over the top of the 'stormy' stories. Use the coloured papers to add more 'sunny' thoughts about the 'sunny' newspaper stories.

Can the groups see any direct matches between the stories, such as a 'stormy' story about over-use of the world's resources and a 'sunny' story about a new recycling campaign?

Leave the newspaper montages on the tables; they may be useful as a prayer focus.

Sharing a meal together

Bring homemade cakes and biscuits to share with drinks after worship. Homemade foods can be a great comfort and represent a gift of time.

Ideas for reflection, prayer and sung worship

Reflection

While everyone stands around the various newspaper montages of 'stormy' and 'sunny' stories, encourage the group to look at the dark centre of the table where the storms are raging in their greyscale world. Many people are affected by these storms of life, so ask God to be with them and to give them strength to weather the storms.

Ask everyone to take a step closer to the table and look at the 'sunny' stories—the bright colours of the papers and the positive words. Invite people to focus on the colours of the sunny stories, letting those colours dominate what they see and allowing the darkness of the stormy pictures to fade away. Thank God for the sunny stories and the hope that they bring.

Sing the hymn 'Father I place into your hands' (JP; MP; RS; TS).

As the singing takes place, mix the stories together—the storms of life with the sunny times of life. Light a candle and place it in the centre of the pictures.

At the end of the singing, draw the prayer to a close by saying that God is in the midst of our lives and we can draw our strength from him.

Prayer suggestions: Ice cube prayer

Plan ahead

A large number of ice cubes will be needed for this prayer. Bags of them can be purchased from supermarkets if it is not possible to make the quantity needed. On the day of worship, the bags of ice cubes can be stored in a fridge or, if it is cold enough, outside the building until the time they are needed for the prayer.

Pray together

When everyone is gathered, light a candle and place a bowl of lukewarm water in a central position, either on a table or on the floor. Have other bowls, filled with the ice cubes, placed around the worship area.

Ask everyone to think of one concern that they would like to bring to God. When each person is ready, they can collect an ice cube, tell their concern or worry to God (out loud or silently) and then float their ice cube on the water to represent their prayer. They then return to their place. As the ice cubes melt, they symbolise our worries disappearing.

When everyone has floated their own ice cubes, float others for the people included in your prayers of intercession.

Sing the first verse of 'Be still, for the presence of the Lord' (CH; JP; MP; TS).

End the prayer by saying the words, 'And all the people said: Amen.'

Hymns and songs

- Autumn days when the grass is jewelled (JP)
- Brother, sister, let me serve you (CH; RS)
- Will your anchor hold in the storms of life? (CH; MP; HP; RS)
- Lord, for the years your love has kept and guided (CH; MP; RS; TS)
- Be bold, be strong (JP; MP; TS)
- Father, I place into your hands (JP; MP; RS; TS)
- Jesus, we celebrate the victory (MP; TS)
- Though the earth should (TS)

Taking it further

Have a dedicated space in the church for people to bring stories, clippings and notes. Divide the space into 'stormy' and 'sunny' stories.

*

— Theme 11 —

Following traditions

Suggested month
November

Season of the year
Autumn

Christian season
Advent

Colour
Purple

Theme introduction

November arrives as the last threads of autumn give way to winter. The leaves have been torn from the trees by strong winds and collect in heaps at the side of the road. The afternoons are short and night-time creeps up on us soon after we have finished our lunch. The colours of autumn have subsided, making way for a grey and brown landscape that lies bare in the elements.

In the United Kingdom, Guy Fawkes Night is celebrated on 5 November. Families have their own traditions: some people light a bonfire in the garden and eat potatoes cooked in their jackets, others attend a fireworks display in their local park and have toffee apples, and some draw their names in the dark sky with their 'sparkler' wands. Hot punch, cinder toffee, parkin and sizzling sausages are all foods traditionally associated with Guy Fawkes Night.

Town and village centres, schools, libraries, leisure centres and shops will all be embarking on the annual tradition of decorating windows and interiors in anticipation of the coming season of Christmas. However, for many people, the time of Advent simply passes them by!

Church life is very busy at this time of year. In each local church, thoughts are turning to familiar traditions regarding Advent and Christmas. Some churches will have a Christmas fair, which takes lots of planning and includes both new and traditional ideas. Groups will be thinking ahead to decorations, visits and Christmas parties, using their own traditions as the starting point for their activities.

Traditions are funny things. Sometimes they just go on and on without too much thought being given to them. In some families and churches, the phrase 'We always do it that way' is often heard and there is a delight in carrying on those customs, but sometimes it is good to stop and think about the traditions we all hold dear. (Or do we?)

Using the Old Testament as a starting point, this theme encourages your church to look at its traditions and understand where they have come from. What do long-established traditions mean to the current worshipping community? What might they mean to people who are new to the church? Asking questions such as 'Why do we do this?' and 'What do we mean by this?' (and others, stimulated by group members) will help a church to have a better understanding of why things are done the way they are and to embrace their traditions, or perhaps consign some of them to history. NB: Such discussions should be held in a sensitive manner because what might not be important to one person may be very important to another.

As the theme moves to a conclusion, people will be encouraged to consider what their legacy will be, in leaving traditions for the future. Who decides what those traditions will be, and what could they mean to the people who will inherit them in the years to come?

Biblical context

A child has been born for us. We have been given a son who will be our ruler. His names will be Wonderful Adviser and Mighty God, Eternal Father and Prince of Peace. His power will never end; peace will last for ever. He will rule David's kingdom and make it grow strong. He will always rule with honesty and justice. The Lord All-Powerful will make certain that all of this is done.

ISAIAH 9:6–7

So John went along the Jordan Valley, telling the people, 'Turn back to God and be baptised! Then your sins will be forgiven.' Isaiah the prophet wrote about John when he said, 'In the desert someone is shouting, "Get the road ready for the Lord! Make a straight path for him. Fill up every valley and level every mountain and hill. Straighten the crooked paths and smooth out the rough roads. Then everyone will see the saving power of God."'

LUKE 3:3–6

I have already told you what the Lord Jesus did on the night he was betrayed. And it came from the Lord himself. He took some bread in his hands. Then after he had given thanks, he broke it and said, 'This is my body, which is given for you. Eat this and remember me.' After the meal, Jesus took a cup of wine in his hands and said, 'This is my blood, and with it God makes his new agreement with you. Drink this and remember me.'

1 CORINTHIANS 11:23–25

Reflection

In the Old Testament, the book of Isaiah is littered with passages that have been interpreted by many Christians as references to the birth of Christ in the New Testament. In the first of the passages above, Isaiah tells the people of the birth of a baby who is yet to come. He is preparing them for something that will happen in the future and for what the coming of God's chosen Saviour will mean to them.

The second passage is from Luke's Gospel. It records Jesus' cousin, John, calling the people to prepare, to be ready for the coming of Christ. John is reminding the people of what the prophet Isaiah had said long before.

Both Isaiah and John are telling us to 'get ready' and to 'prepare'—and this is what Advent is all about.

The third reading is from Paul's first letter to the church in Corinth. In this passage, Paul reminds the Corinthian church that when Jesus shared bread and wine with his disciples as symbols of his own body and blood, he asked them to remember him whenever they ate bread and drank wine in this way. By this we see that Jesus created the tradition of Holy Communion.

All three passages are, in some way, about tradition and the reasons why we have them. Preparing, being ready and remembering are all important activities that help us to feel part of places and communities. Every now and again, we should take a good look at the traditions we uphold and be clear about their purpose. We must make sure that we do not find ourselves in the situation of the Pharisees, to whom Jesus said, 'You have a fine way of setting aside the commands of God in order to observe your own traditions!' (Mark 7:9, NIV).

Theme exploration

To set the scene, have a display area draped with a purple cloth. Add items that relate to the world around us and some traditional foods for this time of year.

A tree for Advent

Plan ahead

Set up a Christmas tree, with only the lights in place (but not turned on), in a position where it will remain throughout the Advent and Christmas celebrations. Provide a variety of decorations to be hung on the tree: they could be new decorations or ones that have been used before. Have enough for everyone to be able to hang one on the tree.

Decorate the tree

As people arrive for worship on the first Sunday in Advent, invite them to choose one of the decorations and keep it with them until they can place it on the tree. Begin worship by playing a piece of music or singing a favourite carol. Invite people to decorate the tree as the music is played or the carol is sung.

Other decorations may be added on each Sunday in Advent until the tree is fully decorated. On the last Sunday before Christmas, add the star at the top of the tree and switch on the lights.

Advent ring

If you have the tradition of an Advent ring in your church, follow this tradition but spend time talking about the symbolism attached to the candles.

Different denominations and churches have various reasons for lighting each candle, and the colours of the candles can vary, too.

Advent banners

Plan ahead

Four Advent banners can be made, either all in advance or one by one during the season of Advent, to be hung week by week as they are ready. In future years, they will be available to reuse in worship throughout the weeks of Advent.

The banners can either depict the story of Christmas, each decorated with a different Christmas symbol, or each one can depict a single candle. Whichever design is chosen, the banners are placed in the church, one at a time, on each Sunday throughout Advent.

Candle banners

Using heavyweight fabric with a satin finish, which gives a shine, make four large banners, each measuring approximately one metre by two metres. If you want the candle images to be coloured, use a white fabric for the background. If the candle images are to be white, use a coloured background fabric (such as purple).

Make a casing at the top of each banner for a pole or cane to pass through, so that the banner can be hung up. A similar casing can be made at the bottom of the banner, so that a cane can be sealed in to the base to give added weight.

Using a basic candle design, cut out a fabric candle in a suitable size to fit in the centre of the satin background while leaving a reasonable margin around the candle to frame the image. Sew or glue the candle in place. When each banner is completed, fix a cane or rod through the casing at the top of the hanging and secure another one through the bottom casing if the banner is to be weighted.

Hang one candle banner for each Sunday in Advent, beginning with the first Sunday and continuing until all four banners are hung.

'Story of Christmas' banners

Decide what image to place on each banner for each of the four Sundays in Advent. The images need to be large and simple, so that they are easy to produce in fabric and can be seen from a distance. Images might include:

- A candle: representing Jesus—the light for the world.
- Three crowns: representing the three wise men (magi or kings).
- An angel: representing the annunciation, and also the message to the shepherds.
- Trumpets: representing the heavenly host.
- The manger: where the infant Jesus was laid after he was born.
- A star: representing the star that the wise men followed.

When the images have been chosen, decide on the colours to be used. Choose colours that work well together but also make the images stand out. The backing fabrics could all be one colour—for example, purple, red or green—and the images could be in gold, white or black, or a mixture of all three. Alternatively, the backing fabrics could all be different and the images all the same colour. As with the candle banners above, the backing fabric needs to be approximately one metre by two metres in size.

Sew or glue the images in place on the background. When the banners are completed, fix a cane or rod through the casing at the top and bottom as described above.

Display one banner on the first Sunday in Advent and then display an additional banner on each of the subsequent Sundays in Advent. These banners could form the basis of weekly worship themes throughout Advent.

Age-specific theme activities

Countdown pass-the-parcel

Age guide: Under 5
Aim: To enjoy the sense of anticipation

Plan ahead

Prepare a pass-the-parcel package made with 24 layers. Label each layer of wrapping with a number, 1 on the very outside and 24 on the inside as the last layer. The gift at the centre should be a symbol to represent Jesus. This could be part of a nativity figure set, a Christmas storybook or something else that represents the story of Jesus' birth, such as a decorative star—whatever seems appropriate.

Small objects representing parts of the Christmas story or characters from the nativity could be placed inside the sixth, twelfth and 18th wrappers. This will mean that something may be 'won' on each Sunday through Advent and that the different events in the story are told to help build the anticipation. Have a plate of mini sugar gem biscuits or little sweets to share at the end, each time the game is played.

Play the game

Play a game of countdown pass-the-parcel each Sunday throughout Advent, removing six wrappers every time.

Each week, talk about the different traditions that the children enjoy about Christmas. Also talk about the pass-the-parcel game and about how we are counting down to a special event. Explain what and who we are waiting for. Be mindful of the ages and abilities of those in the group and only take the conversation as far as it is possible to go, bearing these factors in mind.

Advent stars

Age guide: Under 10
Aim: To make decorations for the tree

Plan ahead

Have enough pre-cut stars or baubles (round gift tabs make good bauble shapes) for each child to make a decoration for the church tree and also have one to take home.

Prepare a selection of sequins, tissue paper for scrunching, honeycomb paper and other craft pieces to decorate the stars and baubles.

Make the decorations

As the children create their decorations, talk about the traditions in their own homes. What do they enjoy and what helps them to think about the real meaning of Christmas?

Traditions

Age guide: Over 10
Aim: To look afresh at our traditions and why we have them

Divide into small groups. Begin by talking about people's own childhood traditions in Advent and Christmas and then about traditions in the homes of children today. On a large piece of paper, write each tradition and the reason why it continues to be followed.

Start a discussion on the traditions in the church during Advent. Think about things that happen both inside the church and beyond its walls, such as carol singing around the neighbourhood or holding a charity Christmas card sale in the town. Discuss the traditions that the church follows as Christmas draws near. Again, on a large piece of paper, make a list of the traditions, with a note of when and why they take place. If there is a tradition that has been passed down and no one in the group knows why (guessing is not allowed), try to find out why—other members of the church family may know.

If it is not possible to discover why a certain tradition is followed, write it on a separate list.

Talk about who is the 'keeper' of each tradition—for example, 'The Ladies' Circle always decorates the church for Christmas' or 'Mr Brown always brings the tree'—and why that is so. There could be very good reasons or it could be that people no longer know: they just say, 'It's always done that way!' Do these traditions need to change or is everyone happy with the current expectations? Are Mr Brown and the Ladies' Circle happy with the arrangement? These questions should be asked in a sensitive way, not a challenging way.

If there are traditions on the list that have an unknown origin or people are not really sure why they exist any longer, talk about whether or not they should continue. Care needs to be taken in the discussion so that people do not feel challenged in a negative way. If it is decided that an established tradition should be stopped, plan to do so for one year initially. If the tradition is missed, it is probably better to reinstate it. Make sure everyone is consulted before changing things.

All-age theme activities

A new tradition

Aim: To begin a new tradition to carry forward into the future

This activity is suitable for all ages working together. You will need some packs of gift tags, a mini tree (such as a wooden mug tree) and a basket.

Arrange the gift tags in the basket and the mini tree in a central position in the room. Place the sheets from the 'Traditions' activity above in a visible position so that people can refer to them if they wish.

Invite people to think of something they would like to happen as part of the Advent celebrations at your church. This should be anything that would enhance the preparations of the worshipping community—for example, hanging Christmas banners through the weeks of Advent or having a singing group brought together for Advent.

Write the possible new traditions on the gift tags, read them out and then hang them on the mini tree. Place the tree in the display area and allow the ideas on the tree to flow around the room and work through people's minds.

Decide over lunch which, if any, of the suggestions may become new traditions. The suggestions could be tried out and a decision made later.

As the discussion takes place about possible new traditions, think about how the worshipping community will view the new traditions. Is it clear why each activity is to take place, and does it honour God in the way it should?

Sharing a meal together

Have lunch with everyone bringing some items that they enjoy sharing.

Ideas for reflection, prayer and sung worship

Reflection

Place images or a model of the nativity in a central place, clearly visible. You could use images or models that are created as part of this session or brought in specially for this reflection.

Focus people's thoughts with these words.

- Look at images of the nativity scene. Think about what they mean to you.
- Think about the familiarity of the characters of the nativity.
- Think about the tradition they hold as they are placed before us.
- Now imagine yourself in the nativity itself, on that night when the characters gathered for the very first time.
- The scene was new; it was fresh; it was exciting and full of hope.
- Think about the smell of the straw, the heat from the animals and the noises as people passed by outside.
- Look at the nativity once more.
- Remember how important its tradition is to you.

Finish with a prayer.

Prayer suggestions

During the intercessions, as prayers are spoken for ourselves, our neighbours and the world, invite the church to hum the tune of 'Silent night, holy night' or another quiet carol of your choice. The contrast between the spoken words of the prayer and the unspoken words of the carol makes quite an impact. When the prayers have finished, allow the humming to continue to the end of a verse and then say 'Amen'.

Hymns and songs

- O come, O come, Immanuel (CH; MP; JP; HAM; HP; RS)
- Make way, make way, for Christ the King (CH; JP; MP; RS; TS)
- Who would think that what was needed (CH; RS)
- Christmas is coming! The church is glad to sing (CH)
- Joy to the world, the Lord is come (RS; MP; HP; RS; TS)
- Long ago, prophets knew (HAM; HP)

Taking it further

Nativity pass-the-parcel

Prepare a countdown pass-the-parcel (see p. 132) for the whole church to share in an act of worship. The parcel needs to be made with enough layers to hide several different characters of the nativity story. A slip of paper should be placed with each character, on which is written his or her part of the story. Prayers and carols can also be included in the parcel. As the parcel is passed around the church, the characters' stories will emerge and worship will evolve. The success of the parcel is in the planning!

Traditions around the world

Aim: To discover the traditions of other countries

Research traditions from other parts of the world and create a display, adding the stories of other traditions to the display throughout Advent. These can be stories discovered from the internet, from books or from people who have travelled to different places in the season of Advent and Christmas. For example, a church in Boston, USA, is filled with poinsettia plants throughout Advent, one for every family connected with the church. With around 500 plants, the church is ablaze with colour as the plants are placed in every conceivable place. On the days between the fourth Sunday in Advent and Christmas Day, church members take the plants to the families for which they were pledged or bought, so everyone is visited by their church friends during those few days.

Sending Advent greetings

Aim: To share the time of preparation with those outside the church

Focus on local community buildings such as local shops, schools, post office, library and other churches. Make and send Advent greeting cards telling the story of Advent. Explain the purpose of Advent as a time of preparation for Christmas, to help people understand the true meaning of Christmas. Send the Advent greetings cards to people with whom the church already has a connection, such as the head teacher of a local school, or to new people, such as the staff of the local post office.

Encourage the local press to run a feature once a week through Advent, showing a picture of each of your four Advent banners and the part of the story they represent. In future years, perhaps the banners could tour key community places and be visible throughout Advent in public places.

Christmas

Suggested month
December

Season of the year
Winter

Christian season
Christmas

Colour
White or gold

Theme introduction

December brings us to the end of the year. All around us, the natural world is sleeping, sometimes hushed by a blanket of snow and frequently silenced by the harsh winter weather. The shortest day of the year is in December and occasionally daylight is barely visible at all. However, we are warmed by the glow of lights from inside the houses, the Christmas scents that fill the shops and the promise of the birth of Jesus, coming into our midst on Christmas Eve.

This theme looks at the story of Christmas, piecing together the events as they are told to us through the Old and New Testaments. Some parts of the story are very familiar to us but others are not always remembered, having become less popular with our hymn writers or with those who write Christmas plays and stories. Like the sleepy natural world, they have been hushed or silenced in the mists of time.

Through a variety of readings, activities and games, we explore the story of Christmas and the roots of some of its traditions, and we begin thinking about what Christmas means in today's environment.

This theme takes us on a quest to discover anew the true meaning of Christmas.

Biblical context

About that time Emperor Augustus gave orders for the names of all the people to be listed in record books. These first records were made when Quirinius was governor of Syria. Everyone had to go to their own home town to be listed. So Joseph had to leave Nazareth in Galilee and go to Bethlehem in Judea. Long ago Bethlehem had been King David's home town, and Joseph went there because he was from David's family.

Mary was engaged to Joseph and travelled with him to Bethlehem. She was soon going to have a baby, and while they were there, she gave birth to her firstborn son. She dressed him in baby clothes and laid him on a bed of hay, because there was no room for them in the inn.

That night in the fields near Bethlehem some shepherds were guarding their sheep. All at once an angel came down to them from the Lord, and the brightness of the Lord's glory flashed around them. The shepherds were frightened. But the angel said, 'Don't be afraid! I have good news for you, which will make everyone happy. This very day in King David's home town a Saviour was born for you. He is Christ the Lord. You will know who he is, because you will find him dressed in baby clothes and lying on a bed of hay.'

Suddenly many other angels came down from heaven and

joined in praising God. They said: 'Praise God in heaven! Peace on earth to everyone who pleases God.' After the angels had left and gone back to heaven, the shepherds said to each other, 'Let's go to Bethlehem and see what the Lord has told us about.' They hurried off and found Mary and Joseph, and they saw the baby lying on a bed of hay. When the shepherds saw Jesus, they told his parents what the angel had said about him. Everyone listened and was surprised. But Mary kept thinking about all this and wondering what it meant.

As the shepherds returned to their sheep, they were praising God and saying wonderful things about him. Everything they had seen and heard was just as the angel had said.

LUKE 2:1–20

When Jesus was born in the village of Bethlehem in Judea, Herod was king. During this time some wise men from the east came to Jerusalem and said, 'Where is the child born to be king of the Jews? We saw his star in the east and have come to worship him.' When King Herod heard about this, he was worried, and so was everyone else in Jerusalem. Herod brought together the chief priests and the teachers of the Law of Moses and asked them, 'Where will the Messiah be born?'

They told him, 'He will be born in Bethlehem, just as the prophet wrote, "Bethlehem in the land of Judea, you are very important among the towns of Judea. From your town will come a leader, who will be like a shepherd for my people Israel."' Herod secretly called in the wise men and asked them when they had first seen the star. He told them, 'Go to Bethlehem and search carefully for the child. As soon as you find him, let me know. I want to go and worship him too.'

The wise men listened to what the king said and then left. And the star they had seen in the east went on ahead of them until it stopped over the place where the child was. They were thrilled and excited to see the star. When the men went into the house and saw the child with Mary, his mother, they knelt down and worshipped him. They took out their gifts of gold, frankincense, and myrrh and gave them to him. Later they were warned in a dream not to return to Herod, and they went back home by another road.

After the wise men had gone, an angel from the Lord appeared to Joseph in a dream and said, 'Get up! Hurry and take the child and his mother to Egypt! Stay there until I tell you to return, because Herod is looking for the child and wants to kill him.' That night, Joseph got up and took his wife and the child to Egypt, where they stayed until Herod died. So the Lord's promise came true, just as the prophet had said, 'I called my son out of Egypt.'

When Herod found out that the wise men from the east had tricked him, he was very angry. He gave orders for his men to kill all the boys who lived in or near Bethlehem and were two years old and younger. This was based on what he had learned from the wise men.

MATTHEW 2:1–16

The two Bible passages above will be read later in the worship.

Theme exploration

To set the scene, have a display area draped with a white or gold cloth. Add something that relates to the world around us, such as a twig with no leaves, a picture of a house at night with the lights shining, or a lantern to represent the shortest day of the year.

Telling the story

This activity is to be done in small groups, either working in mixed-age groups or age-specific groups. Make available pens and paper, or a large sheet of paper fastened to the wall and flipchart pens.

Ask the group what they remember of the Christmas story. Explain that this is not a test, just one way of discovering their collective memory of this particular story. After a brief discussion, ask for someone to be the scribe and ask the group to order what they remember into a sequence of events. There will be a mixture of experiences of the Christmas story among the group, so a mutual respect needs to be encouraged and quieter voices heard, so that everyone is able to join in with the activity.

When each group is happy with their retelling of the Christmas story, ask them to read the Bible passages relating to Jesus' birth (see above).

Ask the following questions.

- Is the group happy with their version of the story?
- What are the differences between their version of the story and the Bible version?
- What are the key points of the Christmas story?

Reflection

The accounts in Luke 2:1–20 and Matthew 2:1–16 are both about the same event but are told from different perspectives. Luke's Gospel begins with the birth of Jesus' cousin, John. The miracle of John's conception and the joy of his parents are shared, and it is clear that God's hand is guiding events as they unfold. Luke 1 ends with the words, 'As John grew up, God's Spirit gave him great power' (v. 80). It is with this knowledge that the scene is set for the coming of Jesus in Luke 2.

However, the entrance of the New Testament's principal character is not like that of a leading actor, who is expected to carry off the show. It presents a baby—a newborn child, hungry and needing comfort like every other baby. Luke 2:8–20 is devoted to the amazing events that took place in a field outside Bethlehem, where angels appeared to shepherds to tell them about Jesus' birth. The shepherds were so amazed that they went to see this special baby for themselves and, after seeing him, shared the good news of his birth with others.

In Matthew's Gospel, time is spent in the first chapter giving an account of the ancestral line of Jesus. Joseph's encounter with an angel, who tells him that Mary is pregnant, is in the second part of this passage, and Jesus arrives at the very end of the chapter. Matthew 2 begins with the story of wise men travelling great distances to see the new 'king of the Jews' (v. 2). Unfortunately, they were looking in the wrong place and evoked the wrath of King Herod, who ordered the death of all the infant boys in the district so that his sovereignty could not be challenged. The wise men took gifts to the new king and protected him by not returning to Herod to report the baby's whereabouts.

Taking it deeper

The prophecy

Have written out on separate cards the following passages from Isaiah: 9:6–7; 11:1–9; 40:3–5; 40:9–10; 52:7–10; 52:13; 53:12. Number the cards in sequence so that the readings will be read out in order.

Place the cards face down on a table or on the floor and ask for volunteers to take a card and find the passage in the Bible. Read the quotes in sequence order. This could be done in pairs, with one person finding the passage and the other reading it out.

Ask the group members to decide what they think are the key points from the passages. Discuss the following:

- Did Isaiah's prophecy live up to expectations?
- If Isaiah had been able to visit the baby in the manger, do you think he would have been surprised by the way his prophecy had become reality?

- If Isaiah's prophecy had been broadcast on the evening news earlier this year, what would be our expectations today?

Compare Isaiah's prophecy with the Gospel accounts of Jesus' birth. Draw out the parallels between the stories.

Christmas carol competition

Aim: To have fun remembering and singing Christmas carols

Divide into four or six groups of mixed ages. One person will need to be a scribe and keep a record of carols sung. You will also need two judges, preferably of different generations, as some carols will be traditional and some will be contemporary.

Rules

- Everyone in the group must listen to each other's suggestions about which carol to sing.
- Everyone in the group must sing the suggested carol if they are able to do so.
- When a carol has been sung once, it cannot be sung again by any of the groups.
- Only carols may be sung—popular songs are not carols!

Each group sits in a different part of the worship space. Number the groups (alternatively, the groups can come up with a name for their group). Taking it in turns, each group sings the first verse of a carol. Turns are taken in the same order for each round to ensure that everyone participates. The judges decide whether the song is a popular song or a carol, and the scribe keeps a list of all the carols sung in the game. Groups drop out when they can't think of a different carol to sing. The game ends when everyone runs out of ideas.

At the end of the game, ask the scribe to count up how many

carols were sung in total. The group that sang the most carols is the winning group and may be awarded a small prize. Finally, everyone celebrates the combined score with a round of applause.

Age-specific theme activities

The nativity

Age guide: Under 5
Aim: To make a nativity scene and understand the roles of the characters

Either make or use a model of the nativity, or use play figures purchased from a toy shop that could be cast as figures in the nativity scene. Tell the story of Jesus' birth and encourage the children to play with the figures as you speak. Pause from time to time in the storytelling to allow the game to play out. (Be prepared for some creative additions to the biblical telling of the story.) At the end of the story, talk about what happened and use the figures to create a tableau of the final scene in the nativity.

Christmas angels

Age guide: Under 10
Aim: To make biscuits to share

Most children enjoy cooking, so use a simple shortbread biscuit recipe of your choice to make the biscuits. It is probably best if the children work in pairs, so have enough ingredients for each pair to make at least two biscuits each.

When the mixture is made, roll it out using a rolling pin and, using an angel-shaped cutter or a card template of an angel, carefully cut out the biscuits. If the biscuits are to be hung on a tree, make a hole, not too close to the top, for ribbon to be threaded through after the biscuits are cooked and cooled. Using a pallet knife, carefully move the biscuits on to a greased baking tray and bake them until light brown in colour (according to your recipe instructions). As the biscuits are being made, talk about the Christmas story and the role the angels played in the story. When the biscuits are cool, they can be eaten, shared with the rest of the church (see suggestion below), hung on the Christmas tree or taken home.

Christmas crackers

Age guide: Over 10
Aim: To relate the Christmas story by making connections with life today

This activity is to be done either in age-specific groups or in small mixed-age groups. Either make or bring enough Christmas crackers for each group to have one each. Place inside each cracker one of the following questions. (If there are too many questions, be selective.) You may wish also to write your own questions.

- Mary and Joseph had to travel to Joseph's home town for a census ordered by their government. Who makes the rules that we live by in the world, the country, our place of work, our schools and our homes? Are they always fair?
- Mary and Joseph had a long journey to Bethlehem. How would we complete such a journey today? What preparations would be needed for the journey?
- When Jesus was born, Mary and Joseph took care of him. Who takes care of us when we need to be looked after? Who do we care for?
- If Jesus was born today, would he be recognised as a king? What qualities are needed to be a king or queen?
- God sent angels to tell the good news of Jesus' birth to the shepherds. Angels also told Joseph what he had to do to keep

Jesus and Mary safe. Where do we get good advice from and who are our 'angels'?

- The shepherds came to celebrate Jesus' birth. What present would we have taken to Jesus if we had been able to visit him?
- There was no room for Mary and Joseph to stay in the inn so, when Mary gave birth to Jesus, she wrapped him in cloths and laid him in a manger (Luke 2:7, NIV). Who are the vulnerable people in today's world? (Think about those who are homeless, immigrants, young people, children, elderly people, asylum seekers and so on.)
- Wise men travelled a great distance to see Jesus. Who do we deem to be wise men and women today? Who do we look to as leaders? (Think about friends, parents, grandparents, teachers, celebrities and so on.)
- Herod did not want Jesus to survive because he saw him as a threat. Do we have enemies? When is it right to run away and when is it right to stand up to them?
- Mary and Joseph took Jesus to Egypt to escape from Herod. Who are our refugees today? Why do people become refugees?

Before the activity begins, nominate one person to be the leader of each group. His or her role is to keep the conversation going and to ensure that everyone who wishes to comment is able to do so. Give one cracker to each group. When the group is ready to begin, two people pull the cracker and the question will fall out. The group members then discuss the question for ten minutes. After ten minutes the groups share their questions and responses with each other. If time allows and more crackers are prepared, the groups could move on to a second cracker question.

NB: Care will need to be given to ensure that all views are heard. Also, all participants should be reminded to be respectful of other's viewpoints, which might be different from their own.

Sharing a meal together

Choose from one of the following options. Some will involve more planning than others.

- After the worship, have a time of drinks and biscuits. Provide tea, coffee and soft drinks and enjoy them with the angel biscuits made earlier, or with Christmas biscuits or mince pies.
- Plan in advance to have lunch together. This could be a picnic lunch or a shared lunch. Talk about the events leading up to Jesus' birth (it is likely that Mary and Joseph had food with them to eat on their journey and when they arrived in Bethlehem).
- Have Christmas dinner together. This will take a great deal of planning but, with everyone helping and contributing, it should be possible. Celebrate the true meaning of Christmas by sharing this meal together.

Ideas for reflection, prayer and sung worship

Reflection

Make Christingles to celebrate God's gifts. The word 'Christingle' means 'Christ-light'. The first Christingle service was held on Christmas Eve in 1747 at Marienborn in Moravia. The children were encouraged to take their Christingle home and relight it on their windowsills to show the light of Christ to passers-by.

A Christingle is an orange pierced with four cocktail sticks, upon which are placed small sweets or candied fruit. A candle is then pushed into the top and a red ribbon tied around the middle of the orange. Symbolically, the orange represents God's love in the world; the cocktail sticks represent God's love in the seasons; the sweets or fruits represent God's love in providing the fruits of the earth; the candle represents God's love in sending Jesus, who is the light for the world; and the ribbon represents God's love through Jesus' death and resurrection.

Provide enough materials for everyone to make a Christingle for themselves. Have help available for those who need it and take care when handling the cocktail sticks. Talk about what each part of the Christingle means as you put it together and reflect on the symbolism of the items used.

1. Start with the orange, which represents the world.
2. Add the candle, which symbolises Jesus Christ, who is the light for the world.
3. Place the four cocktail sticks around the candle to represent the four seasons.
4. Add sweets or candied fruit to the sticks to symbolise God's love in providing the fruits of the earth.
5. Tie a red ribbon around the middle of the orange (or secure it with sticky tape) as a reminder of Jesus' death and resurrection.

When the Christingles are made, invite everyone to sit or stand in a circle. The candles can be lit and carols sung. Choose carols that most people will know so that printed words are not needed. Finally, encourage everyone to take their Christingle home and to light the candle and display the Christingle in a safe place.

Prayer suggestions

Use a published prayer resource to guide the prayers.

Give everyone a star (packs of pre-cut sparkly stars are available from stationers or craft suppliers) and ask them to write on the back of the star something from today's worship that they wish to pray about. Pass a basket around for everyone to put their prayers in and place the basket in the centre of the room. Finish with a collective prayer, offering the star prayers to God.

Hymns and songs

- Joy to the world (CH; MP; HP; RS; TS)
- See him lying on a bed of straw (CH; JP; MP; HP; RS)
- Go, tell it on the mountain (JP; MP; HP; RS)
- Born in the night (JP; MP; HP; RS)
- Who would think that what was needed (CH; RS)
- In the bleak midwinter (CH; HAM; MP; HP; RS)

Christingle songs

- Can you see what we have made? (TS)
- It's rounded like an orange (CH; JP)
- Bring your Christingle with gladness and joy (CH; JP)

Taking it further

- Create a life-sized stable to represent where Jesus was born, and hold worship among bales of hay around a manger. In rural locations, it may be possible to visit a farm and have your worship in a barn surrounded by lowing cattle.
- Invite another church to an evening of sharing. Use the Christmas carol game and the meal suggestions as a start to planning the evening.

*

Bible index

Old Testament

Genesis 1:27–30 106
Genesis 8:22 106
Numbers 20:6–11 27
Psalm 78:1–7 60–61
Isaiah 9:6–7 127

New Testament

Matthew 2:1–16 141–142
Matthew 6:5–15 72–73
Matthew 14:14–21 84–85
Matthew 14:22–23 95
Matthew 26:26–30 37
Mark 1:35–37 95
Mark 6:31–32 95
Mark 15:33–39 50
Mark 16:1–8 50–51
Luke 2:1–20 140–141
Luke 3:3–6 127
Luke 8:22–25 116
Luke 12:22–31 116
Luke 22:19–20 37–38
Luke 24:36–49 51
Romans 12:4–8 16
1 Corinthians 11:23–25 127

✳

Resources

Creative Ideas for Quiet Corners by Lynn Chambers (Barnabas, 2008)

The Lord's Prayer Unplugged by Lucy Moore (Barnabas, 2004)

The Barnabas Children's Bible by Rhona Davies (Barnabas, 2007)

Bethlehem Carols Unplugged by Lucy Moore and Martyn Payne (Barnabas, 2008)

Good as New: A Radical Retelling of the Scriptures by John Henson (O Books, 2004)

Messy Church by Lucy Moore (Barnabas, 2006)

The Strong Towers: Stories for Tough Times by Robert Harrison and Roger Langton (Scripture Union, 2006)

Prayer and meditation resources

Each Day and Each Night: Celtic Prayers by J. Philip Newell (Wild Goose Publications, 2002)

Entertaining Angels by Geoffrey Duncan (Canterbury Press, 2005)

Growing Hope by Neil Paynter (Wild Goose Publications, 2006)

Our story wall hanging

Single block

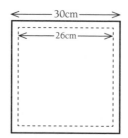

Finished wall hanging

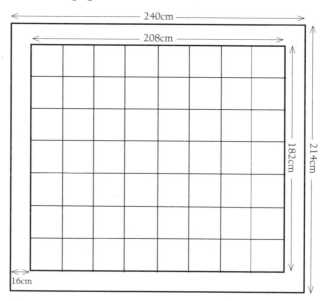

Creative Ideas for Quiet Corners

14 visual prayer ideas for quiet moments with children

Lynn Chambers

One of the most significant responsibilities of any Christian parent, godparent, grandparent or children's work leader is to help children to learn what it means to speak and listen to God through prayer. Yet space for prayer is often, at best, pushed into a corner.

This book offers 14 creative suggestions designed to encourage both adults and children to find space for prayer, by creating a physical prayer space in the home or in a place of worship that can be visited and enjoyed. The materials could be used to form an ongoing sacred space throughout the months of the year or offered at particular times—for example, during a school holiday or a season of the year such as Christmas or Easter.

Each prayer idea uses simple, easily found materials and needs minimal space to create a quiet, reflective corner. All the materials have been carefully chosen to nurture an understanding of what it means to come into the presence of God, to listen and to be still. Alongside the visual tableaux, the book offers practical support to enable people of all ages and abilities to move at their own pace and at their own level into a sense of quietness and prayer.

ISBN 978 1 84101 546 0   £6.99
Available from your local Christian bookshop or, in case of difficulty, direct from BRF using the order form on page 159.

All-Age Worship

Lucy Moore

'Noooooo!' The prospect of all-age worship can produce a cry of anguish from many people. It's time to admit that arranging worship with all ages present is easy to do appallingly and difficult to do well. But it's also time to admit that a church which unthinkingly packs any group, old or young, off to worship and learn in another space every week could well be completely daft...

This book is for those who sense that worshipping God together is probably a good thing, but are nervous of trying to lead their church towards that. It acknowledges that we don't live in a perfect world—or church—and that no one has all the answers. It also argues that you are the expert for the ways in which your church can best worship God, and helps you start to find those ways and adapt them for your local setting.

ISBN 978 1 84101 432 6 £7.99
Available from your local Christian bookshop or, in case of difficulty, direct from BRF using the order form on page 159.

Messy Church

Fresh ideas for building a Christ-centred community

Lucy Moore

Messy Church is bursting with easy-to-do ideas to draw people of all ages together and help them to experience what it means to be part of a Christian community outside Sunday worship.

At its heart, *Messy Church* aims to create the opportunity for parents, carers and children to enjoy expressing their creativity, sit down together to eat a meal, experience worship and have fun within a church context.

The book sets out the theory and practice of *Messy Church* and offers 15 themed programme ideas to get you started, each including:

- Bible references and background information
- Suggestions for 10 easy-to-do creative art and craft activities
- Easy-to-prepare everyday recipes
- Family-friendly worship outlines

ISBN 978 1 84101 503 3   £8.99
Available from your local Christian bookshop or, in case of difficulty, direct from BRF using the order form on page 159.

The Barnabas Children's Bible

Rhona Davies

Illustrated by Marcin Piwowarski

This new Children's Bible includes stories chosen to cover all the main events, retold with a continuous thread.

There are 365 stories, one for every day of the year, each accompanied by Bible quotations from a real Bible translation, giving readers a taste of the language and style of the original texts.

The stylish illustrations illuminate and inform, while the easily accessible encyclopedia at the end of the book helps to explain the context and background of the stories. All combine to make this a useful and readable Bible for children.

ISBN 978 1 84101 526 2   £12.99
Available from your local Christian bookshop or, in case of difficulty, direct from BRF using the order form on page 159.

ORDERFORM

REF	TITLE	PRICE	QTY	TOTAL
546 0	Creative Ideas for Quiet Corners	£6.99		
432 6	All-Age Worship	£7.99		
503 3	Messy Church	£8.99		
526 2	The Barnabas Children's Bible	£12.99		

POSTAGE AND PACKING CHARGES					Postage and packing	
Order value	UK	Europe	Surface	Air Mail	Donation	
£7.00 & under	£1.25	£3.00	£3.50	£5.50	TOTAL	
£7.10–£30.00	£2.25	£5.50	£6.50	£10.00		
Over £30.00	FREE	prices on request				

Name _____ Account Number _____

Address _____

_____ Postcode _____

Telephone Number_____

Email _____

Payment by: ❑ Cheque ❑ Mastercard ❑ Visa ❑ Postal Order ❑ Maestro

Card no ❑❑❑❑ ❑❑❑❑ ❑❑❑❑ ❑❑❑❑ ❑❑❑

Valid from ❑❑❑❑ Expires ❑❑❑❑ Issue no. ❑❑❑

Security code* ❑❑❑ *Last 3 digits on the reverse of the card.
ESSENTIAL IN ORDER TO PROCESS YOUR ORDER   Shaded boxes for Maestro use only

Signature _____ Date _____

All orders must be accompanied by the appropriate payment.

Please send your completed order form to:
BRF, 15 The Chambers, Vineyard, Abingdon OX14 3FE
Tel. 01865 319700 / Fax. 01865 319701 Email: enquiries@brf.org.uk

❑ Please send me further information about BRF publications.

Available from your local Christian bookshop.   BRF is a Registered Charity

About
brf:

BRF is a registered charity and also a limited company, and has been in existence since 1922. Through all that we do—producing resources, providing training, working face-to-face with adults and children, and via the web—we work to resource individuals and church communities in their Christian discipleship through the Bible, prayer and worship.

Our Barnabas children's team works with primary schools and churches to help children under 11, and the adults who work with them, to explore Christianity creatively and to bring the Bible alive.

To find out more about BRF and its core activities and ministries, visit:

www.brf.org.uk
www.barnabasinschools.org.uk
www.barnabasinchurches.org.uk
www.messychurch.org.uk
www.foundations21.org.uk

If you have any questions about BRF and our work, please email us at

enquiries@brf.org.uk